Robert's
RULES OF ORDER

Robert's
RULES OF ORDER

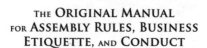

THE ORIGINAL MANUAL
FOR ASSEMBLY RULES, BUSINESS
ETIQUETTE, AND CONDUCT

—— Henry Robert ——

Foreword by Chris MacDonald, PhD

CLYDESDALE

First published in 1892 by S. C. Griggs & Company

First Skyhorse Publishing Edition 2017

Clydesdale Press books may be purchased in bulk at special discounts for sales promotion, corporate gifts, fund-raising, or educational purposes. Special editions can also be created to specifications.F or details, contact the Special Sales Department, Skyhorse Publishing, 307 West 36th Street, 11th Floor, New York, NY 10018 or info@skyhorsepublishing.com.

Clydesdale Press® is a registered trademark of Skyhorse Publishing, Inc.®, a Delaware corporation.

Visit our website at www.skyhorsepublishing.com.

10 9 8 7 6 5 4 3 2

Library of Congress Cataloging-in-Publication Data is available on file.

Print ISBN: 978-1-945186-40-0
Ebook ISBN: 978-1-945186-41-7

Printed in the United States of America

TABLE OF CONTENTS.

TABLE OF CONTENTS.

Part II. — Organization and Conduct of Business.

FOREWORD

It goes without saying that *Robert's Rules* is a classic of parliamentary procedure. As has commonly been pointed out, *Robert's Rules* has been enormously influential, adopted since its first publication in 1876 by a wide variety of organizations of all kinds, both across the United States and well beyond. What is less commonly pointed out is the work's philosophical richness. But to a philosopher and scholar of ethics like myself, *Robert's Rules* is inevitably read as a work of practical ethics, a real-life implementation of the notion of a social contract, the mythical foundational agreement regarding how we are to live together about which so much philosophical ink has been spilled. From a practical point of view, it is an attempt to find a set of rules conducive to the well-being of communities, a way to pursue the common good while paying due attention to balancing the needs of those communities with the rights of individuals.

Perhaps the lack of attention to the book's philosophical significance is not surprising. The book's near obsessive attention to detail risks masking the moral import of the work. And *Robert's Rules* is nothing if not thorough. It is exhaustive in its contemplation of the contingencies of deliberation, thorough in its provision of rules and sub-rules for dealing with them, and relentless in its cross-referencing. Guidance is provided about how individuals may make proposals (i.e. motions), how and when they may amend those motions, and the limits to be placed on amendment and debate. It provides, for example, that motions may be made and amended, and that amendments themselves may be amended, but that amendments to amendments may not. You may wonder why an assembly even needs such a rule. But Robert, in his wisdom, foresaw the need, and included a rule about it.

Henry Martyn Robert was a soldier and military engineer from South Carolina. Legend has it that, once upon a time, he was called upon to chair a meeting of his local Baptist church. The meeting, it is said, did not go well. The discussion was chaotic and not entirely polite, and Robert was embarrassed about his failure to guide it along a more fruitful path. But Henry Martyn Robert, recall, was an engineer, and so in the need for a more fruitful discussion he saw a design challenge, the need to build a better mousetrap, so to speak. So with an engineer's eye to both form and function, he set out to create a set of procedures—drawing upon US congressional practice and the rules of English-style parliaments more generally—designed generically to guide an assembly, aimed at a collective purpose, in its attempt to work collegially.

Some of the rules in the volume serve what seem to

be purely pragmatic purposes. These include for example the deceptively simple, fundamental rule that a *motion* must precede any *discussion*. This principle inevitably saves time and anguish by ensuring that the matter under consideration at any given moment—specifically the action being proposed—is clear to all involved in the discussion. Under the guidance of this principle, there is no question of enduring hours' worth of debate on later to find that participants were talking past each other, ultimately disagreeing over just what the proposal was in the first place. Such a rule is bound to increase efficiency.

Other rules serve clear and obvious moral purposes. Take, for instance, the rule (in Section 46, on Voting) that "no one can vote on a question in which he has a direct personal or pecuniary interest." This is a succinct rule for dealing with what, today, we would call "conflict of interest." If someone is allowed to vote on a matter from which they stand to benefit in a material way, there is every possibility that narrow interest will affect his or her judgment in ways that are unfair to the common interest and perhaps in ways that even the individual him- or herself would not, in a moment of calm reflection, endorse.

The careful attention that *Robert's Rules* plays to questions of leadership, on the other hand, bridges the practical and the moral. A fundamental challenge for deliberative bodies, and one to which *Robert's Rules* pays considerable attention, is the need for leadership that is powerful enough to be useful, but limited enough to be trusted. *Robert's Rules* thus outlines carefully the role and responsibilities of the Chairman or President, but also explains the procedure for appealing the Chairman or President's ruling, and the situations in which such appeal is possible.

Ultimately, *Robert's Rules* is a grand recognition of the importance of the rule of law—or, perhaps more aptly, the rule of rules. It is an assertion of the eternal moral principle that the joint action and deliberation of a community must be ruled, not by the wisdom, let alone whim, of an individual, but by a set of rules agreed to in some sense by the entire community. And, crucially, those rules must not be secret, not held closely by the learned few, but rather published and shared with the many. The fact that the rules are published means that every member of the assembly may know them and is thereby enabled to hold the chair to account. In this regard, Robert is clear that a good part of the value of a set of procedural rules lies in their mere existence. The members of a deliberative body will no doubt always be aware that there are other, perhaps equally good ways of carrying out deliberation. But they will benefit from the fact that a set of rules exists, and is known to them, in the first place. "These may not be the best rules, but they are *our* rules."

The need for a volume like *Robert's Rules* points to a profound human need, namely the need that humans have to come together in pursuit of shared goals. The impetus to live in community, to solve shared problems, and to build more together than they could build individually requires not just common ends, but common means. The need for joint deliberation, in other words, and for joint action, is unquestionable. The mechanism for achieving this effectively is not.

In order for joint deliberation to be effective, certain conditions must obtain—conditions that *Robert's Rules* seeks to establish for any deliberative body willing to follow the book's advice. First, and most importantly, the success of any deliberative assembly requires that there be at least a partial subordination of individual interests to the interests of the group. The group cannot function if each individual continually attempts to put his or her own interests first. Hence, the *Rules* provide that in order to obtain the consent of the group, an individual member must put forward a motion, have it seconded by another, and ultimately persuade a majority to agree. Second, and as a corollary to the first condition, the individual's interest must not be *entirely* subordinated. Each individual participant must retain the belief that he or she will be heard and that the collective deliberation is a way to advance his or her own interests, even if only through compromise rather than entirely to frustrate them. Hence, the *Rules* stipulate both that members are entitled to be heard and that there is a means of appealing the decision of the chair when an individual feels aggrieved. And finally, joint deliberation to be effective, there must be a mechanism for balancing the interests of individuals, under circumstances in which each wants to speak—whether to express his or her own interests or to express his or her vision of the common good—but all cannot speak at once.

In this regard, *Robert's Rules* constitute an exercise in

what philosophers call procedural justice. The focus on procedure is, at one level, a recognition that substantive justice—justice of outcomes—is often elusive. Divide the pie one way, and I feel wronged. Divide it another way, and you do. We may never agree on the best way to divide the pie. But, if we are a little bit lucky and a little bit wise, we might strike upon a decent procedure for making the decision, such that once a decision is made, even if the parties to the decision cannot all be equally satisfied with it, each must at least admit that the process that got them there was fair. In the end, of course, deliberative assemblies are tasked with deciding what is to be done. *Robert's* does not pretend to tell us what goals an assembly should have. Robert's gift to us, rather, is a common answer to the question, "How will we decide?"

For these reasons, as you read, study, and put *Robert's Rules* into action, I encourage you to see it as more than a set of rules or instructions. It is, at heart, a vote for the ultimate rationality of human beings and their fundamental ability to come together in pursuit of shared goals. A set of rules, yes, but a set of rules that, once accepted, leaves us freer and more able than before. Where some see constraints, we ought to see the roots of liberty.

—**Chris MacDonald, PhD,**
editor of *The Concise Encyclopedia of Business Ethics*

TABLE OF RULES
RELATING TO MOTIONS.

———

[If information is desired in reference to a motion, look first in this Table, which decides seven points in regard to each motion, and also shows the section in the Manual treating fully of each, thus serving as an index of motions. A list of the motions belonging to each of the seven classes indicated by the headings to the columns, can be found by noticing the stars in each column.

The motions are classified into Principal, Subsidiary, Incidental and Privileged in §§ 6–9. The common motions are classified in § 55 according to the object for which each is used. If other information is required about motions in general, look in the Index under the title *Motions*.]

TABLE OF RULES RELATING TO MOTIONS.

[Containing Answers to Two Hundred Questions in Parliamentary Practice.]

Explanation of the Table.—A Star shows that the rule heading the column in which it stands, applies to the motion opposite to which it is placed; a cipher shows that the rule does not apply; a figure shows that the rule only partially applies, the figure referring to the note showing the limitations. Take, for example, "Lie on the Table;" the Table shows that § 19 of the Pocket Manual treats of this motion; that it is "undebatable" and "cannot be amended;" and that an affirmative vote on it (as shown in note 5) "cannot be reconsidered;"—the four other columns containing ciphers show that this motion does not "open the main question to debate," that it does not "require a ⅔ vote," that it does not "require to be seconded," and that it is not "in order when another member has the floor."

Section in Pocket Manual.		Undebatable [§ 35].	Opens Main Question to Debate [§ 35].	Cannot be Amended [§ 23].	Cannot be Reconsidered [§ 27].	Requires a ⅔ Vote [§ 39].—See Note 1.	Does not require to be Seconded [§ 3].	In order when another has the floor [§ 2].
11	Adjourn	*	0	*	*	0	0	0
10	Adjourn, Fix the Time to which to.	2	0	0	0	0	0	0
23	Amend [3].	0	0	0	0	0	0	0
23	Amend an Amendment.	0	0	0	0	0	0	0
45	Amend the Rules.	0	0	*	0	0	0	0
14	Appeal, relating to indecorum, etc. [4].	*	0	0	0	*	0	*
14	Appeal, all other cases.	0	0	0	0	0	0	*
14	Call to Order.	*	0	0	0	0	*	*

NOTES.

(1) Every motion in this column has the effect of suspending some rule or established right of deliberative assemblies (as shown in the note to § 39), and therefore requires a two-thirds vote, unless a special rule to the contrary is adopted.

(2) Undebatable if made when another question is before the assembly.

(3) An Amendment may be either (1) by "adding," or (2) by "striking out" words or paragraphs; or (3) by "striking out certain words and inserting others," or (4) by "substituting" a different motion on the same subject; or (5) by "dividing the question" into two or more questions, as specified by the mover, so as to get a separate vote on any particular point or points.

(4) An Appeal is undebatable only when relating to indecorum, or to transgressions of the rules of speak-

87	Close Debate, motion to	*	0	0	0	0	0	0	ing, or to the priority of business, or when made while the Previous Question is pending. When debatable, only one speech from each member is permitted. On a tie vote the decision of the Chair is sustained.
22	Commit	0	*	0	0	0	0	0	
34	Extend the Limits of Debate, motion to	*	0	0	0	0	0	0	
10	Fix the time to which to Adjourn	2	0	0	0	0	0	0	
36	Leave to Continue Speaking after Indecorum	0	*	0	0	0	0	0	
19	Lie on the Table	0	0	5	0	0	0	0	
37	Limit Debate, motion to	*	0	0	*	0	0	0	
15	Objection to Consideration of a Question [6]	0	0	0	0	*	*	*	(5) An affirmative vote on this motion cannot be reconsidered.
13	Orders of the Day, motion for the	0	0	0	0	*	0	*	(6) The objection can only be made when the question is first introduced, before debate.
21	Postpone to a Certain Time	7	0	0	0	0	0	0	
24	Postpone Indefinitely	0	*	0	0	0	0	0	(7) Allows of but limited debate upon the propriety of the postponement.
20	Previous Question [8]	*	0	0	0	0	0	0	(8) The Previous Question, if adopted, cuts off debate and brings the assembly to a vote on the pending question only, except where the pending motion is an amendment or a motion to commit, when it also applies to the question to be amended or committed.
44	Priority of Business, questions relating to	*	0	0	0	0	0	0	
12	Privilege, Questions of	0	0	0	0	0	0	0	
16	Reading Papers	0	0	0	0	0	0	0	
27	Reconsider a Debatable Question	*	0	0	0	0	9	0	
27	Reconsider an Undebatable Question	*	0	0	0	0	9	0	
22	Refer (same as Commit)	0	*	0	0	0	0	0	
11	Rise (in Committee equals Adjourn)	*	0	0	0	0	0	0	(9) Can be moved and entered on the record when another has the floor, but cannot interrupt business then before the assembly; must be made on the day the original vote was taken, and by one who voted with the prevailing side.
15	Shall the Question be Discussed ? [6]	0	0	0	0	*	0	0	
13	Special Order, to make a	0	0	0	0	0	0	0	
28	Substitute (same as Amend)	*	0	0	5	0	0	0	
18	Suspend the Rules	*	0	0	0	0	0	0	
19	Take from the Table	*	0	0	0	0	0	0	
44	Take up a Question out of its Proper Order	*	0	0	0	0	0	0	
17	Withdrawal of a Motion	0	*	0	0	0	0	0	

See next page for *Order of Precedence of Motions and Forms of Putting Certain Questions.*

ADDITIONAL RULES TO ACCOMPANY TABLE.

Order of Precedence of Motions.

The ordinary motions rank as follows, and any of them (except to amend) can be made while one of a lower order is pending, but none can supersede one of a higher order:

To Fix the Time to which to Adjourn.
To Adjourn (when unqualified).
For the Orders of the Day.
To Lie on the Table.
For the Previous Question.
To Postpone to a Certain Time.
To Commit.
To Amend.
To Postpone Indefinitely.

The motion to Reconsider can be made when any other question is before the assembly, but cannot be acted upon until the business then before the assembly is disposed of [see note 9 above], when, if called up, it takes precedence of all other motions except to adjourn, and to fix the time to which to adjourn. Questions incidental to those before the assembly, take precedence of them and must be acted upon first.

Forms of Putting Certain Questions.

If a motion is made to *Strike out* certain words, the question is put in this form: "Shall these words stand as a part of the resolution?" so that on a tie vote they are struck out.

If the *Previous Question* is demanded, it is put thus: "Shall the main question be now put?"

If an *Appeal* is made from the decision of the Chair, the question is put thus: "Shall the decision of the Chair stand as the judgment of the assembly [convention, society, etc.]?"[*]

If the *Orders of the Day* are called for, the question is put thus: "Will the assembly now proceed to the Orders of the Day?"

When, upon the introduction of a question, some one *objects to its consideration*, the chairman immediately puts the question thus: "Will the assembly consider it?" or "Shall the question be considered [or discussed]?"

If the vote has been ordered to be taken by *yeas and nays*, the question is put in a form similar to the following: "As many as are in favor of the adoption of these resolutions, will, when their names are called, answer *yes* [or *aye*] — those opposed will answer *no*."

PREFACE.

A work on parliamentary law has long been needed, based, in its general principles, upon the rules and practice of Congress, but adapted, in its details, to the use of ordinary societies. Such a work should give not only the methods of organizing and conducting meetings, the duties of officers and names of ordinary motions, but should also state systematically in reference to each motion, its object and effect; whether it can be amended or debated; if debatable, the extent to which it opens the main question to debate; the circumstances under which it can be made, and what other motions can be made while it is pending. This Manual has been prepared with a hope of supplying the above information in a condensed and systematic form, each rule in Part I either being complete in itself, or giving references to every section that in any way qualifies it, so that a stranger to the work can refer to any special subject with safety.

A Table of Rules is placed immediately before this Preface, which will enable a presiding officer to decide some two hundred common and important questions of parliamentary law without turning a page.

The Second Part is a simple explanation of the common methods of conducting business in ordinary meetings. The motions are classified here according to their uses, and those used for a similar purpose are compared with each other. This part is intended for that large class in every community who are almost wholly unacquainted with parliamentary usages and are not able to devote much study to the subject, but would be glad with little labor to learn enough to enable them to take part in meetings of deliberative assemblies without fear of being out of order.

The Third Part contains some useful information, including the legal rights of assemblies, call of the house, etc.

The object of Rules of Order is to assist an assembly to accomplish the work for which it was designed, in the best possible manner. To do this it is necessary to restrain the individual somewhat, as the right of an individual in any community, to do what he pleases, is incompatible with the interests of the whole. Where there is no law, but every man does what is right in his own eyes, there is the least of real liberty. Experience has shown the importance of definiteness in the law; and in this country, where customs are so slightly established and the published manuals of parliamentary practice so conflicting, no society should attempt to conduct business without having adopted some work upon the subject, as the authority in all cases not covered by their own special rules.

It has been well said by one of the greatest of English writers on parliamentary law: "Whether these forms be in all cases the most rational or not is really not of so great importance. It is much more material that there should be a rule to go by, than what that rule is, that there may be a uniformity of proceeding in business, not subject to the caprice of the chairman, or captiousness of the members. It is very material that order, decency and regularity be preserved in a dignified public body."

H. M. R.

INTRODUCTION.

Parliamentary Law.

Parliamentary Law refers originally to the customs and rules of conducting business in the English Parliament; and thence to the customs and rules of our own legislative assemblies. In England these usages of Parliament form a part of the unwritten law of the land, and in our own legislative bodies they are of authority in all cases where they do not conflict with existing rules or precedents.

But as a people we have not the respect which the English have for customs and precedents, and are always ready for such innovations as we think are improvements, and hence changes have been and are constantly being made in the *written* rules which our legislative bodies have found best to adopt. As each house adopts its own rules, it results that the two houses of the same legislature do not always agree in their practice; even in Congress the order of precedence of motions is not the same in both houses, and the Previous Question is admitted in the House of Representatives, but not in the Senate. As a consequence of this, the exact method of conducting business in any particular legislative body is to be obtained only from the Legislative Manual of that body.

The vast number of societies, political, literary,

scientific, benevolent and religious, formed all over the land, though not legislative, are deliberative in character, and must have some system of conducting business, and some rules to govern their proceedings, and are necessarily subject to the common parliamentary law where it does not conflict with their own special rules. But as their knowledge of parliamentary law has been obtained from the usages in this country, rather than from the customs of Parliament, it has resulted that these societies have followed the customs of our own legislative bodies, and our people have thus been educated under a system of parliamentary law which is peculiar to this country, and yet so well established as to supersede the English parliamentary law as the common law of ordinary deliberative assemblies.

The practice of the National House of Representatives should have the same force in this country as the usages of the House of Commons have in England, in determining the general principles of the common parliamentary law of the land; but it does not follow that in every matter of detail the rules of Congress can be appealed to as the common law governing every deliberative assembly. In these matters of detail, the rules of each House of Congress are adapted to their own peculiar wants, and are of no force whatever in other assemblies. But upon all great parliamentary questions, such as what motions can be made, what is their order of precedence, which can be debated, what is their effect, etc., the common law of the land is settled by the practice of the United States House of Representatives, and not by that of the English Parliament, the United States Senate, or any other body.

While in extreme cases there is no difficulty in deciding the question as to whether the practice of Congress determines the common parliamentary law, yet between these extremes there must necessarily be a large number of doubtful cases upon which there would be great difference of opinion, and to avoid the serious difficulties always arising from a lack of definiteness in the law, every deliberative assembly should imitate our legislative bodies in adopting Rules of Order for the conduct of their business.*

---

* Where the practice of Congress differs from that of Parliament upon a material point, the common law of this country follows the practice of Congress. Thus in every American deliberative assembly having no rules for conducting business, the motion to adjourn would be decided to be undebatable, as in Congress, the English parliamentary law to the contrary notwithstanding; so if the Previous Question were negatived, the debate upon the subject would continue as in Congress, whereas in Parliament the subject would be immediately dismissed; so too the Previous Question could be moved when there was before the assembly a motion either to amend, to commit, or to postpone definitely or indefinitely, just as in Congress, notwithstanding that, according to English parliamentary law, the Previous Question could not be moved under such circumstances.

When the rules of the two Houses of Congress conflict, the House of Representatives rules are of greater authority than those of the Senate in determining the parliamentary law of the country, just as the practice of the House of Commons, and not the House of Lords, determines the parliamentary law of England. For instance, though the Senate rules do not allow the motion for the Previous Question, and make the motion to postpone indefinitely take precedence of every other subsidiary motion [§ 7] except to lie on the table, yet the parliamentary law of the land follows the practice of the House of Representatives,

Plan of the Work.

This Manual is prepared to partially meet this want in deliberative assemblies that are not legislative in their character. It has been made sufficiently complete to answer for the rules of an assembly until they see fit to adopt special rules conflicting with and superseding any of its rules of detail, such as the Order of Business [§ 44], etc. Even in matters of detail the practice of Congress is followed, wherever it is not manifestly unsuited to ordinary assemblies;

---

in recognizing the Previous Question as a legitimate motion, and assigning to the very lowest rank the motion to postpone indefinitely.

But in matters of detail, the rules of the House of Representatives are adapted to the peculiar wants of that body, and are of no authority in any other assembly. No one, for instance, would accept the following House of Representatives rules as common parliamentary law in this country: That the chairman, in case of disorderly conduct, would have the power to order the galleries to be cleared; that the ballot could not be used in electing the officers of an assembly; that any fifteen members would be authorized to compel the attendance of absent members and make them pay the expenses of the messengers sent after them; that all committees not appointed by the Chair would have to be appointed by ballot, and if the required number were not elected by a majority vote, then a second ballot must be taken in which a plurality of votes would prevail; that each member would be limited in debate upon any question to one hour; that a day's notice must be given of the introduction of a bill, and that before its passage it must be read three times, and that without the special order of the assembly it cannot be read twice the same day. These examples are sufficient to show the absurdity of the idea that the rules of Congress in all things determine the common parliamentary law.

and in such cases, in Part I, there will be found, in a foot note, the Congressional practice. In the important matters referred to above, in which the practice of the House of Representatives settles the common parliamentary law of the country, this Manual strictly conforms to such practice.*

The Manual is divided into three distinct parts, each complete in itself, and a Table of Rules [see

---

* On account of the party lines being so strictly drawn in Congress, no such thing as harmony of action is possible, and it has been found best to give a bare majority in the House of Representatives (but not in the Senate) the power to take final action upon a question without allowing of any discussion. In ordinary societies more regard should be paid to the rights of the minority, and a two-thirds vote be required, as in this Manual, for sustaining an objection to the introduction of a question, or for adopting a motion for the Previous Question, or for adopting an order closing or limiting debate. [See note to § 39 for a discussion of this question.] In this respect the policy of the Pocket Manual is a mean between those of the House and Senate. But some societies will doubtless find it advantageous to follow the practice of the House of Representatives, and others will prefer that of the Senate. It requires a majority, according to this Manual, to order the yeas and nays [§ 38], which is doubtless best in most assemblies; but in all bodies in which the members are responsible to their constituents, a much smaller number should have this power. In Congress it requires but a one-fifth vote, and in some bodies a single member can require a vote to be taken by yeas and nays.

Any society adopting this Manual should make its rules govern them in all cases to which they are applicable, and in which they are not inconsistent with the By-Laws and Rules of Order of the society. [See § 49 for the form of a rule covering this case.] Their own rules should include all of the cases where it is desirable to vary from the rules in the Manual, and especially should provide for a Quorum [§ 43] and an Order of Business [§ 44], as suggested in these rules.

page 8] containing a large amount of information in a tabular form, for easy reference in the midst of the business of a meeting.

Part I contains a set of Rules of Order systematically arranged, as shown in the Table of Contents. Each one of the forty-five sections is complete in itself, so that one unfamiliar with the work cannot be misled in examining any particular subject. Cross references are freely used to save repeating from other sections, and by this means the reader, without using the index, is referred to everything in the Rules of Order that has any bearing upon the subject he is investigating. The references are by sections, and for convenience the numbers of the sections are placed at the top of each page. The motions are arranged under the usual classes, in their order of rank, but in the Index under the word *motion* will be found an alphabetical list of all the motions generally used.

The following is stated in reference to each motion:

(1) Of what motions *it takes precedence* (that is, what motions may be pending, and yet it be in order to make this motion).

(2) To what motions it *yields* (that is, what motions may be made while this motion is pending).

(3) Whether it is *debatable* or not (all motions being debatable unless the contrary is stated).

(4) Whether it can be *amended* or not.

(5) In case the motion can have no subsidiary motion *applied* to it, the fact is stated [see Adjourn, § 11, for an example: the meaning is, that the particular

motion to adjourn, for example, cannot be laid on the table, postponed, committed or amended].

(6) The *effect* of the motion if adopted, whenever it could possibly be misunderstood.

(7) The *form of stating the question* when peculiar, and all other information necessary to enable one to understand the question.

Part II is a Parliamentary Primer, giving very simple illustrations of the methods of organizing and conducting different kinds of meetings, stating the very words used by the chairman and speakers in making and putting various motions; it also gives briefly, the duties of the officers, and forms of minutes, and of reports of the treasurer and committees; it classifies the motions into eight classes according to their object, and then takes up separately each class and compares those in it, showing under what circumstances each motion should be used.

Part III consists of a few pages devoted to miscellaneous matters that should be understood by members of deliberative assemblies, such as the important but commonly misunderstood subjects of the Legal Rights of Deliberative Assemblies and Ecclesiastical Tribunals, etc.

Definitions and Common Errors.

In addition to the terms defined above (*taking precedence of*, *yielding to* and *applying to*, see p. 18), there are other terms that are liable to be misunderstood, to which attention should be called.

Meeting and *Session*. For the distinction between these terms, see first note to § 42.

Previous Question. The effect of this much mis-understood motion is briefly stated in the eighth note to the Table of Rules, p. 8; a full explanation is given in § 20.

Substitute. This motion is one form of an amend-ment. The five forms of an amendment are shown in the third note to the Table of Rules, p. 8, and are more fully explained in § 23.

Shall the Question be Discussed? is a common form in some societies of stating the question on the con-sideration of a subject. It is very apt to convey a wrong impression of its effect, which is, if negatived, to dismiss the question for that session, as shown in § 15.

Accepting a Report, which is the same as adopting it, is confounded by many with receiving a report. [See note to § 30 for common errors in acting upon reports.]

The terms *Congress* and *H. R.*, when used in this Manual, refer to the U. S. House of Representatives.

The word *Assembly*, when occurring in forms of motions (as in an Appeal, § 14), should be replaced by the special term used to designate the particular assembly — as, for instance, " Society," or " Conven-tion," or " Board."

PART I.

RULES OF ORDER.*

— • —

Art. I. Introduction of Business.

[§§ 1–5.]

1. All business should be brought before the assembly by a motion of a member, or by the presentation of a communication to the assembly. It is not usual, however, to make a motion to receive the reports of committees [§ 30] or communications to the assembly; and in many other cases in the ordinary routine of business, the formality of a motion is dispensed with; but should any member object, a regular motion becomes necessary.

2. Before a member can make a motion or

---

* If the reader's knowledge of the elementary details of parliamentary practice is not sufficient for him to understand these rules in Part I, he should, before proceeding further, read Part II, which is essentially a Parliamentary Primer [See the first note to § 46].

address the assembly upon any question, it is necessary that he **obtain the floor**; that is, he must rise and address the presiding officer by his title, thus: "Mr. Chairman," who will then announce the member's name.* Where two or more rise at the same time, the Chairman must decide who is entitled to the floor, which he does by announcing that member's name. In making his decision he should be guided by the following principles:

(*a*) The member upon whose motion the subject under discussion was brought before the assembly (or, in case of a committee's report, the one who presented the report,) is entitled to be recognized as having the floor (if he has not already had it during that discussion), notwithstanding another member may have first risen and addressed the chair. (*b*) No member who has once had the floor is again entitled to it while the same question is before the assembly, provided the floor is claimed by one who has not spoken to that

---

* If the Chairman has some other title, as President, Moderator, etc., he is addressed by his special title, thus: "Mr. President" [See § 34]. If the Chairman rise to speak before the floor has been assigned to any one, it is the duty of a member who may have previously risen to take his seat. [See Decorum in Debate, § 36.]

question.* (c) As the interests of the assembly are best subserved by allowing the floor to alternate between the friends and enemies of a measure, the Chairman, when he knows which side of a question is taken by each claimant of the floor, and their claim is not determined by the above principles, should give the preference to the one opposed to the last speaker.

From this decision of the Chairman any two members can make an appeal [§ 14]. Where there is doubt as to who is entitled to the floor, the Chairman can at the first allow the assembly to decide the question by a vote — the one getting the largest vote being entitled to the floor.

After the floor has been assigned to a member he cannot be interrupted by calls for the question,† or by a motion to adjourn, or for any purpose, by either the Chairman or any member, except (a) to have entered on the minutes a motion to reconsider [§ 27]; (b) by

---

* See § 26 for an explanation of what is necessary to technically change the question before the assembly.

† It is a plain breach of order when a member has the floor for any one to call for the question or an adjournment; and the Chairman should protect the speaker in his right to address the assembly.

a call to order [§ 14]; (*c*) by an objection to
the consideration of the question [§ 15]; (*d*)
by a call for the orders of the day [§ 13],* or
(*e*) by a question of privilege that requires immediate action, as shown in § 12.

In such cases the member, when he rises
and addresses the Chair, should state at once
for what purpose he rises, as, for instance, that
he "rises to a point of order."

3. Before any subject is open to debate
[§ 34] it is necessary, first, that a motion be
made; second, that it be seconded (see exceptions below); and third, that it be stated
by the presiding officer.† When the motion
is in writing it shall be handed to the Chairman, and read before it is debated.

This does not prevent suggestions of alterations, before the question is stated by the
presiding officer. To the contrary, much
time may be saved by such informal remarks;
which, however, must never be allowed to
run into debate. The member who offers the
motion, until it has been stated by the presiding officer, can modify his motion, or even

---

* See note at close of § 13.

† Examples of the various forms of making motions are given
in §§ 46, 54. Forms of stating questions will be found in § 65.

withdraw it entirely; after it is stated he can
do neither, without the consent of the assembly [see §§ 5, 17]. When the mover modi-
fies his motion, the one who seconded it can
withdraw his second.

Exceptions : A call for the order of the day,
a question of order (though not an appeal), or
an objection to the consideration of the question [§§ 13, 14, 15], does not have to be seconded; and many questions of routine are not
seconded or even made; the presiding officer
merely announcing that, if no objection is
made, such will be considered the action of
the assembly.

4. All Principal Motions [§ 6], Amendments
and Instructions to Committees, should be in
writing, if required by the presiding officer.
Although a question is complicated, and capable of being made into several questions, no
one member (unless there is a special rule
allowing it) can insist upon its being divided;
his resource is to move that the question be
divided, specifying in his motion how it is to be
divided. Any one else can move, as an amendment to this, to divide it differently.

This *Division of a Question* is really an
amendment [§ 23], and subject to the same

rules. Instead of moving a division of the question, the same result can be usually attained by moving some other form of an amendment. When the question is divided, each separate question must be a proper one for the assembly to act upon, even if none of the others were adopted. Thus, a motion to "commit with instructions," is indivisible; because, if divided, and the motion to commit should fail, then the other motion to instruct the committee would be improper, as there would be no committee to instruct.* The motion to "strike out certain words and insert others," is indivisible, as it is strictly one proposition.

5. After a question has been stated by the

---

* The 46th Rule of the House of Representatives requires the division of a question on the demand of one member, provided "it comprehends propositions in substance so distinct that one being taken away, a substantive proposition shall remain for the decision of the House." But this does not allow a division so as to have a vote on separate items or names. The 121st Rule expressly provides that on the demand of one-fifth of the members a separate vote shall be taken on such items separately, and others collectively, as shall be specified in the call, in the case of a bill making appropriations for internal improvements. But this right to divide a question into items extends to no case but the one specified. The common parliamentary law allows of no division except when the assembly orders it, and in ordinary assemblies this rule will be found to give less trouble than the Congressional one

presiding officer, it is in the possession of the assembly for debate; the mover cannot withdraw or modify it, if any one objects, except by obtaining leave from the assembly [§ 17], or by moving an amendment.*

Art. II. General Classification of Motions.†

[§§ 6-9.]

6. A Principal or Main Question or Motion, is a motion made to bring before the assembly, for its consideration, any particular subject. No Principal Motion can be made when any other question is before the assembly. It takes precedence of nothing,

---

* Rule 40 H. R. is as follows: " After a motion is stated by the Speaker, or read by the Clerk, it shall be deemed to be in the possession of the House, but it may be withdrawn at any time before a decision or amendment." The practice under this rule has been, not to allow a motion to be withdrawn after the previous question has been seconded. This manual conforms to the old parliamentary principle, which is probably better adapted to ordinary societies. In certain organizations it will, doubtless, be found advisable to adopt a special rule like the Congressional one just given.

† In § 54, the ordinary motions will be found classified according to their object.

and yields to all Privileged, Incidental and Subsidiary Questions [§§ 7, 8, 9].

7. Subsidiary or Secondary Motions are such as are applied to other motions, for the purpose of most appropriately disposing of them.* They take precedence of a Principal Question, and must be decided before the Principal Question can be acted upon. They yield to Privileged and Incidental Questions, [§§ 8, 9,] and are as follows (being arranged in their order of precedence among themselves):

Lie on the Table .... See § 19
The Previous Question .... " § 20
Postpone to a Certain Day .... " § 21
Commit ... . " § 22
Amend .... " § 23
Postpone Indefinitely .... " § 24

Any of these motions (except to Amend) can be made when one of a lower order is pending, but none can supersede one of a higher order. They cannot be applied† to

---

* Take, for example, a motion that an appeal lie on the table: to lie on the table is a subsidiary motion enabling the assembly to properly dispose of the appeal; while the appeal is an incidental question, arising out of a decision of the Chair, to which some members objected.

† See page 18 for explanation of some of these technical terms.

one another except in the following cases:
(*a*) the Previous Question applies to the motions to Postpone, without affecting the principal motion, and can, if specified, be applied to a pending amendment [§ 20]; (*b*) the motions to Postpone to a certain day, and to Commit, can be amended; and (*c*) a motion to Amend the minutes can be laid on the table without carrying the minutes with it [§19].

8. Incidental Questions are such as arise out of other questions, and, consequently, take precedence of, and are to be decided before, the questions which give rise to them. They yield to Privileged Questions [§ 9], and cannot be amended.   Excepting an Appeal, they are undebatable; an Appeal is debatable or not, according to circumstances, as shown in § 14.   They are as follows:

Appeal (or Questions of Order) .... See § 14
Objection to the Consideration of a
   Question .... " § 15
The Reading of Papers .... " § 16
Leave to Withdraw a Motion .... " § 17
Suspension of the Rules .... " § 18

9. Privileged Questions are such as, on account of their importance, take precedence of all other questions whatever, and on account

of this very privilege they are undebatable
[§ 35], excepting when relating to the rights
of the assembly or its members, as otherwise
they could be made use of so as to seriously
interrupt business.   They are as follows (being
arranged in their order of precedence among
themselves):

To Fix the Time to which the Assembly
  shall Adjourn..................... See § 10
Adjourn .... " § 11
Questions relating to the Rights and
  Privileges of the Assembly or any of
  its Members .... " § 12
Call for the Orders of the Day....... " § 13

Art. III. Motions and their Order of Precedence.*

[§§ 10–27.]

Privileged Motions.

[§§ 10–13; see § 9.]

10. To fix the time to which the Assembly shall Adjourn.   This motion

---

* For a list of all the ordinary motions, arranged in their order
of precedence, see the Table of Rules, page 10. All the Privileged and Subsidiary ones in this Article are so arranged.

takes precedence of all others, and is in order even after the assembly has voted to adjourn, provided the Chairman has not announced the result of the vote. If made when another question is before the assembly, it is undebatable [§ 35]; it can be amended by altering the time. If made when no other question is before the assembly, it stands as any other principal motion, and is debatable.* The *Form* of this motion is, "When this assembly adjourns, it adjourns to meet at such a time."

11. To Adjourn. This motion (when unqualified) takes precedence of all others, except to "fix the time to which to adjourn," to which it yields. It is not debatable, it cannot be amended or have any other subsidiary motion [§ 7] applied to it; nor can a vote on it be reconsidered. If qualified in any way, it loses its privileged character, and stands as any other principal motion. The motion to adjourn can be repeated if there has been any intervening business, though it be simply pro-

---

* In ordinary societies it is better to follow the common parliamentary law, and permit this question to be introduced as a principal question, when it can be debated and suppressed [§§ 58, 59] like other questions. In Congress it is never debatable, and has entirely superseded the unprivileged and inferior motion to "adjourn to a particular time."

gress in debate [§ 26]. When a committee is through with any business referred to it, and prepared to report, instead of adjourning, a motion should be made " to rise," which motion, in committee, has the same privileges as to adjourn in the assembly [§ 32].

The *Effect upon Unfinished Business* of an adjournment is as follows* [see Session, § 42]:

(*a*) When it does not close the session, the business interrupted by the adjournment is the first in order after the reading of the minutes at the next meeting, and is treated the same as if there had been no adjournment; an adjourned meeting being legally the continuation of the meeting of which it is an adjournment.

(*b*) When it closes a session in an assembly which has more than one regular session each year, then the unfinished business shall be

---

* " After six days from the commencement of a second or subsequent session of any Congress, all bills, resolutions and reports which originated in the House, and at the close of the next preceding session remained undetermined, shall be resumed, and acted on in the same manner as if an adjournment had not taken place."—Rule 136 H. R.   But unfinished business does not go over from one Congress to another Congress. Any ordinary society that meets as seldom as once each year, is apt to be composed of as different membership at its successive meetings as any two successive Congresses, and only trouble would result from allowing unfinished business to hold over to the next yearly meeting.

taken up at the next succeeding session previous to new business, and treated the same as if there had been no adjournment [see § 44 for its place in the order of business]. Provided that, in a body elected for a definite time (as a board of directors elected for one year), unfinished business shall fall to the ground with the expiration of the term for which the board or any portion of them were elected.

(*c*) When the adjournment closes a session in an assembly which does not meet more frequently than once a year, or when the assembly is an elective body, and this session ends the term of a portion of the members, the adjournment shall put an end to all business unfinished at the close of the session. The business can be introduced at the next session, the same as if it had never been before the assembly.

12. Questions of Privilege.* Questions relating to the rights and privileges of the as-

---

* Questions of Privilege must not be confounded with Privileged Questions [§ 9]. Disorder in the gallery, one member opening a window so as to cause a draft, endangering the health of others, charges made against the official character of a member, etc., are examples of questions of privilege.

sembly, or any of its members, take precedence of all other questions, except the two
preceding, to which they yield. If the question is one requiring immediate action it can
interrupt a member's speech. When such a
question is raised the Chairman decides
whether it is a question of privilege or not,
from which decision an appeal [§ 14] can be
taken by any two members.

It is not necessary that the assembly take
final action upon the question of privilege
when it is raised — it may be referred to a
committee [§ 22], or laid on the table [§ 19],
or it may have any other subsidiary [§ 7] motion applied to it, and in such case the subsidiary motion is exhausted on it without affecting the question interrupted by the question
of privilege. As soon as the latter is disposed
of, the assembly resumes the consideration of
the question which it interrupted.

13. Orders of the Day. A call for the
Orders of the Day takes precedence of every
other motion, excepting to Reconsider [§ 27],
and the three preceding, to which latter three
it yields, and is not debatable, nor can it be
amended. It does not require to be seconded,

and it is in order when another member has the floor.*

When one or more subjects have been assigned to a particular day or hour, they become the Orders of the Day for that day or hour, and they cannot be considered before that time, except by a two-thirds vote [§ 39]. And when that day or hour arrives, if called up, they take precedence of all but the three preceding questions [§§ 10, 11, 12] and a reconsideration [§ 27]. Instead of considering them, the assembly may appoint another time for their consideration. If not taken up on the day specified, the order falls to the ground.

The orders of the day are divided into two

---

* Rule 54 H. R. provides that at the close of the morning hour (which is devoted to reports from committees and resolutions) a motion is in order to proceed to "the business on the Speaker's table, and to the orders of the day ;" it then specifies the order in which the business on the Speaker's table shall be considered, and closes thus: " The messages, communications and bills on his table having been disposed of, the Speaker shall then proceed to call the orders of the day." While in Congress it is not in order to interrupt a member to call for the orders of the day, yet it is the practice to permit a member, at the close of the morning hour, even though another member has the floor, to move to proceed to "the business on the Speaker's table, and to the orders of the day." To apply the above principle to ordinary assemblies, it is necessary to allow a motion for the orders of the day to interrupt a member who may have the floor, after the time has arrived for their consideration.

classes,— Special Orders and General Orders,
— the first class always taking precedence
of the latter. *General Orders* can be made
by a majority, by postponing questions to certain times, or by adopting a programme or
order of business for the day or session ; these
General Orders cannot interfere with the established rules of the assembly. A *Special
Order* suspends all the rules of the assembly
that interfere with its consideration at the time
specified,* and it therefore requires a two-
thirds vote to make any question a Special
Order. [This motion is in order whenever a
motion to Suspend the Rules [§ 18] is in
order]. After one Special Order is made for
a certain time, it is not in order to make another Special Order to precede or interfere
with it, but a Special Order can interfere with
General Orders.

When the Orders of the Day are taken up,
it is necessary to take up first the Special Orders, if there are any, and then the General

---

* Thus, if an assembly had a rule like that in § 44 for the order
of business, when the time appointed for the Special Order
arrived, any one could call for the Special Orders, even though
a Committee were reporting at the time ; but the orders of the
day in general could not be called for until all the Committees'
reports had been acted upon.

Orders; in each class the separate questions must be taken up in their exact order, the one first assigned to the day or hour taking precedence of one afterwards assigned to the same day or hour. (A motion to take up a particular part of the Orders of the Day, or a certain question, is not a privileged motion). Any of the subjects, when taken up, instead of being then considered, can be assigned to some other time, a majority being competent to postpone even a Special Order.

The *Form* of this question, as put by the Chair when the proper time arrives, or on the call of a member, is, " Shall the Orders of the Day be taken up ? " or, "Will the assembly now proceed to the Orders of the Day ? "

The *Effect* of an *affirmative vote*, on a call for the Orders of the Day, is to remove the question under consideration from before the assembly, the same as if it had been interrupted by an adjournment [§ 11].

The *Effect* of a *negative vote* is to dispense with the orders merely so far as they interfere with the consideration of the question then before the assembly.

A common case of Orders of the Day is where an assembly has adopted an order of business for the day, specifying the hour at which each question shall be considered. When the hour appointed for taking up the second question has arrived, the Chairman should announce that fact, and, if no one objects, immediately put to vote the questions before the assembly, and state the question next to be considered. Should any member object to this, the Chairman should at once submit to the assembly a question like this: "Will the assembly now proceed to consider [here state the subject], which was assigned to this hour?" While a programme, as here supposed, does not state the fact, yet its very form implies that at the expiration of the time allowed any subject, all the questions then pending shall be put to vote. Still, as it takes a formal vote, except by unanimous consent, to proceed originally to the Orders of the Day, so a formal vote is necessary if any one objects, to take up the next order, and close discussion on the one pending.

Incidental Motions.

[§§ 14–18; see § 8.]

14. Appeal [Questions of Order]. A Question of Order takes precedence of the question giving rise to it, and must be decided by the presiding officer without debate. If a member objects to the decision, he says, " I appeal from the decision of the Chair." If the Appeal is seconded, the Chairman immediately states the question as follows : " Shall the decision of the Chair stand as the judgment of the assembly? "* If there is a tie vote the decision of the Chair is sustained.

This Appeal yields to Privileged Questions [§ 9]. It cannot be amended; it cannot be debated when it relates simply to indecorum [§ 36], or to transgressions of the rules of speaking, or to the priority of business, or if it is made while the previous question [§ 20] is pending. When debatable, no member is allowed to speak but once, and, whether debatable or not, the presiding officer, without leaving the chair, can state the reasons upon which he bases his decision. The motion to Lie on the Table† [§ 19], and the Previous Question [§ 20] if the Appeal is debatable,

---

* The word Assembly can be replaced by Society, Convention, Board, etc., according to the name of the organization. See § 65 for a fuller explanation of the method of stating the question on an Appeal.

† In Congress, the usual course in case of an Appeal is to lay it on the table, as this practically kills it and sustains the Chair.

can be applied to an Appeal, and when adopted they affect nothing but the Appeal. The vote on an Appeal may also be reconsidered [§ 27]. An Appeal is not in order when another Appeal is pending.

It is the duty of the presiding officer to enforce the rules and orders of the assembly, without debate or delay. It is also the right of every member, who notices a breach of a rule, to insist upon its enforcement. In such cases he shall rise from his seat, and say, "Mr. Chairman, I rise to a point of order." The speaker should immediately take his seat, and the Chairman requests the member to state his point of order, which he does, and resumes his seat. The Chair decides the point, and then, if no appeal is taken, permits the first member to resume his speech. If the member's remarks are decided to be improper, and any one objects to his continuing his speech, he cannot continue it without a vote of the assembly to that effect.

Instead of the method just described, it is usual, when it is simply a case of improper language used in debate, for a member to say, "I call the gentleman to order;" the Chairman decides whether the speaker is in or out of order, and proceeds as before. The Chairman can ask the advice of members when he has to decide questions of order, but the advice must be given sitting, to avoid the appearance of debate; or the Chair, when unable to decide the question, may at once submit it to the assembly.

15. Objection to the Consideration of a Question. An objection can be made to the consideration of any principal motion [§ 6], but only when it is first introduced, before it has been debated. It is similar to a question of order [§ 14], in that it can be made while another member has the floor, and does not require a second; and as the Chairman can call a member to order, so can he put this question, if he deems it necessary, upon his own responsibility. It cannot be debated [§ 35], or amended [§ 23], or have any other subsidiary motion [§ 7] applied to it. When a motion is made and any member "objects to its consideration," the Chairman shall immediately put the question, "Will the assembly consider it?" or, "Shall the question be considered [or discussed]?" If decided in the negative by a two-thirds vote [§ 39], the whole matter is dismissed for that session

[§ 42]; otherwise the discussion continues as if this question had never been made.

The *Object* of this motion is not to cut off debate, (for which other motions are provided, see § 37,) but to enable the assembly to avoid altogether any question which it may deem irrelevant, unprofitable or contentious.*

16. Reading Papers. [For the order of precedence, see § 8.] Where papers are laid before the assembly, every member has a right to have them once read before he can be compelled to vote on them, and whenever a member asks for the reading of any such paper, evidently for information, and not for delay,

---

* In Congress, the introduction of such questions could be temporarily prevented by a majority vote under the 41st Rule of the House of Representatives, which is as follows: "Where any motion or proposition is made, the question, 'Will the House now consider it?' shall not be put unless it is demanded by some member, or is deemed necessary by the Speaker." [See note at close of § 39.] The English use the "Previous Question" for a similar purpose [see note at close of § 20].

The question of consideration is seldom raised in Congress, but in assemblies with very short sessions, where but few questions can or should be considered, it seems a necessity that two-thirds of the assembly should be able to instantly throw out a question they do not wish to consider. A very common form, in ordinary societies, of putting this question, is, "Shall the question be discussed?" The form to which preference is given in the rule conforms more to the Congressional one, and is less liable to be misunderstood.

the Chair should direct it to be read, if no one objects. But a member has not the right to have anything read (excepting as stated above) without getting permission from the assembly. The question upon granting such permission cannot be debated or amended.

17. Withdrawal of a Motion. [For order of precedence, see § 8.] When a question is before the assembly and the mover wishes to withdraw or modify it, or substitute a different one in its place, if no one objects, the presiding officer grants the permission; if any objection is made, it will be necessary to obtain leave to withdraw,* etc., on a motion for that purpose. This motion cannot be debated or amended. When a motion is withdrawn, the effect is the same as if it had never been made.

18. Suspension of the Rules. [For the order of precedence, see § 8.] This motion is not debatable, and cannot be amended, nor can any subsidiary [§ 7] motion be applied to it, nor a vote on it be reconsidered [§ 27], nor

---

* In Congress, a motion may be withdrawn by the mover, before a decision or amendment [Rule 40 H. R.]. Nothing would be gained in ordinary societies by varying from the old common law as stated above [See note to § 5].

a motion to suspend the rules for the same purpose be renewed [§ 26] at the same meeting, though it may be renewed after an adjournment, though the next meeting be held the same day.*　The rules of the assembly shall not be suspended except for a definite purpose, and by a two-thirds vote; nor shall any rule be suspended, unless by unanimous consent, that gives any right to a minority as small as one-third.†

The *Form* of this motion is, "to suspend the rules which interfere with," etc., specifying the object of the suspension.

Subsidiary Motions.

[§§ 19–24; see § 7.]

19. To Lie on the Table.　This motion takes precedence of all other Subsidiary Questions [§ 7], and yields to any Privileged [§ 9] or Incidental [§ 8] Question.　It is not debatable, and cannot be amended or have any other subsidiary motion [§ 7] applied to it, nor can an affirmative vote on it be reconsidered

---

* In Congress it cannot be renewed the same day.

† There would be no use in a rule allowing one-fifth of the members present to order the yeas and nays, for instance, if two-thirds of those present could suspend the rule [see the last notes to §§ 38, 39].

[§ 27]. It removes the subject from consideration till the assembly vote to take it from the table.

The *Form* of this motion is, " I move that the question lie on the table," or, " that it be laid on the table," or, " to lay the question on the table." When it is desired to take the question up again, a motion is made, either " to take the question from the table," or " to now consider such and such a question; " which motion is undebatable, and cannot have any subsidiary motion applied to it.

The *Object* of this motion is to postpone the subject in such a way that at any time it can be taken up, either at the same or some future meeting, which could not be accomplished by a motion to postpone, either definitely or indefinitely. It is also frequently used to suppress a question [§ 59], which it does, provided a majority vote can never be obtained to take it from the table during that session [§ 42].

The *Effect* of this motion is in general to place on the table everything that adheres to the subject;* so that if an amendment be or-

---

* A question of privilege [§ 12] does not adhere to the subject it may happen to interrupt, and consequently if laid on the table does not carry with it the question pending when it was raised.

dered to lie on the table, the subject which it is proposed to amend goes there with it. The following cases are exceptional : (*a*) An appeal [§ 14] being laid on the table, has the effect of sustaining, at least for the time, the decision of the Chair, and does not carry the original subject to the table. (*b*) So when a motion to reconsider [§ 27] a question is laid on the table, the original question is left just where it was before the reconsideration was moved. (*c*) An amendment to the minutes being laid on the table does not carry the minutes with it.

Even after the ordering of the Previous Question up to the moment of taking the last vote under it, it is in order to lay upon the table the questions still before the assembly.

20. The Previous Question* takes precedence of every debatable question [§ 35],

---

* The Previous Question is a technical name for this motion, conveying a wrong impression of its import, as it has nothing to do with the subject previously under consideration. To demand the previous question is equivalent in effect to moving "That debate now cease, and the assembly immediately proceed to vote on the pending question" [or "questions" in some cases, as shown above under the *effect* of the previous question]. So when the Chairman puts the question, "Shall the main question be now put?" it means, "Shall the pending question be now put?" [or "questions," as just stated]. The origin of this question, and the changes that have taken place in its effects, are described in the note at the close of this section.

and yields to Privileged [§ 9] and Incidental
[§ 8] Questions, and to the motion to Lie on
the Table [§ 19]. It is not debatable, and
cannot be amended or have any other subsidiary [§ 7] motion applied to it. It applies
to questions of privilege [§ 12] as well as to
any other debatable questions. It is allowable for a member to submit a resolution and
at the same time move the previous question
thereon. It shall require a two-thirds * vote
for its adoption.

When a member calls for the previous
question, and the call is seconded, the presiding officer must immediately put the question, " Shall the main question be now put?"
If it fails, the discussion continues as if this
motion had not been made.

If adopted, its *Effect* is as follows: [See
the illustrations near the close of this section.]

(1) Its effect [excepting when to Amend
or to Commit is pending] is to instantly close

---

* In the House of Representatives it must be seconded by a
majority [to avoid the yeas and nays], and then it can be adopted
by a majority vote ; in the U. S. Senate it is not allowed. It is
sometimes called the " gag law," which name is deserved when a
bare majority can adopt it. The right of debate should be considered as an established rule of every deliberative assembly,
which cannot be interfered with excepting by a vote that is
competent to suspend any other rule. [See note to § 39.]

debate,* and bring the assembly to a vote upon the pending question. This vote being taken, the effect of the previous question is exhausted, and the business before the assembly stands exactly as if the vote on the pending motion had been taken in the usual way, without having been forced to it by the previous question; so if this vote is reconsidered [§ 27] the question is divested of the previous question, and is again open to debate.

(2) Its effect when either of the motions to Amend [§ 23] or to Commit [§ 22] is pending, is to cut off debate, and to force a vote, not only upon the motions to amend and to commit, but also upon the question to be amended or committed.† The Chairman puts to vote all these questions in their order

---

*After debate is closed upon a question which has been reported from a Committee, the member reporting the measure has the right to make the closing speech [see § 34].

† If we consider the motions to amend and to commit as inseparably connected with the question to be amended or committed, so that together they constitute but one question, then it would be correct to say that the only effect of adopting the Previous Question is to cut off debate and to force the assembly to vote upon the *one question pending*. This will to many be the easiest way to look at this question, and it makes it as simple as adopting an order closing debate [§ 37 (*d*)], as the latter would have the same privileges, and therefore the same complications as the Previous Question.

of precedence, beginning with the one last moved [see illustrations further on]. The previous question is not exhausted until votes have been taken on all these questions, or else it has been voted to refer the subject to a committee. If one of these votes is reconsidered before the previous question is exhausted, the pendency of the previous question precludes debate upon the motion reconsidered.

The previous question can be moved on a pending amendment, and if adopted, debate is closed on the amendment only. After the amendment is voted on, the main question is again open to debate and amendments. [In this case the form of the question would be similar to this, "Shall the amendment be now put to the question?"] So in the same manner it can be moved on an amendment of an amendment.

The *Object* of the previous question is to bring the assembly to a vote on the question before it without further debate.*

An Appeal [§ 14] from the decision of the Chair is undebatable [§ 35] if made after the

---

* For other methods of closing debate see §§ 37, 58.]

previous question has been moved, and while it is still pending.

To *Illustrate the Effect* of the previous question under all kinds of circumstances, take the following examples:

(*a*) Suppose a question is before the assembly, and an amendment to it offered, and then it is moved to postpone [§ 21] the question to another time: the previous question now being ordered stops the debate and forces a vote on the pending question — the postponement. When that vote is taken the effect of the previous question is exhausted. If the assembly refuses to postpone the subject, the debate is resumed upon the pending amendment.

(*b*) Suppose the subject under consideration is interrupted by a question of privilege [§ 12], and it has been moved to refer this latter question to a committee: the previous question being now ordered brings the assembly to a vote first on the motion to commit, and, if that motion fails, next on the privileged question. After the privileged question is voted on, the previous question is exhausted, and the consideration of the subject which was interrupted is resumed.

(c) Suppose, again, that, while an amendment to the question is pending, a motion is made to refer the subject to a committee, and some one moves to amend this last motion by giving the committee instructions: in addition to the main question we have here only the motions to amend and to commit, and therefore the previous question, if ordered, applies to them all as one question. The Chairman immediately puts the question (1) on the committee's instructions, (2) on the motion to commit, and if this is adopted the subject is referred to the committee and the effect of the previous question is exhausted; but if it fails, next (3) on the amendment, and finally (4) on the main question.

NOTE ON THE PREVIOUS QUESTION.—Much of the confusion heretofore existing in regard to the Previous Question has arisen from the great changes which this motion has undergone. As originally designed, and at present used in the English Parliament, the previous question was not intended to suppress debate, but to suppress the main question, and therefore, in England, it is always moved by the enemies of the measure, who then vote in the negative. It was first used in 1604, and was intended to be applied only to delicate questions; it was put in this form, " Shall the main question be put?" and being negatived, the main question was dismissed for that session. Its form was afterwards changed to this. which is used at present, " Shall the main ques-

tion be *now* put?" and if negatived the question was
dismissed, at first only until after the ensuing debate
was over, but now, for that day. The motion for the
previous question could be debated; when once put
to vote, whether decided affirmatively or negatively,
it prevented any discussion of the main question, for,
if decided affirmatively, the main question was immediately put, and if decided negatively (that is, that
the main question be not now put), it was dismissed
for the day.

Our Congress has gradually changed the English
Previous Question into an entirely different motion,
so that, while in England the mover of the previous
question votes against it, in this country he votes for
it.   At first the previous question was debatable, and
if it was negatived the main question was dismissed
for the day, as in England. Congress, in 1805, made
it undebatable, and in 1860 caused the consideration
of the subject to be resumed if the previous question
was negatived, thus completely changing it from the
English motion.   At first its effect was to cut off all
motions except the main question, upon which a vote
was immediately taken. This was changed in 1840
so as to bring the House to a vote first upon pending
amendments, and then upon the main question.   In
1848 its effect was changed again so as to bring the
House to a vote upon the motion to commit if it had
been made, then upon amendments reported by a
committee, if any, then upon pending amendments,
and finally upon the main question. In 1860 Congress decided that the only effect of the previous
question, if the motion to postpone were pending,
should be to bring the House to a direct vote on the
postponement — thus preventing the previous question from cutting off any pending motion, and com-
pleting the change this motion had been gradually
undergoing. The previous question is now a simple
motion to close debate and proceed to voting as
described in the above section.

[To prevent the introduction of any improper or

useless subject in an ordinary assembly in this country, the proper course is to "object to its consideration" [§ 15] when it is first introduced, which is very similar to the English previous question.]

21. To Postpone to a Certain Day.

This motion takes precedence of a motion to Commit, or Amend, or Indefinitely Postpone, and yields to any Privileged [§ 9] or Incidental [§ 8] Question, and to the motion to Lie on the Table, or for the Previous Question. It can be amended by altering the time, and the Previous Question can be applied to it without affecting any other motions pending. It allows of very limited debate [§ 35], and that must not go into the merits of the subject matter any further than is necessary to enable the assembly to judge of the propriety of the postponement.

The *Effect* of this motion is to postpone the entire subject to the time specified, until which time it cannot be taken up except by a two-thirds vote [§ 13]. When that time arrives it is entitled to be taken up in preference to everything except Privileged Questions Where several questions are postponed to different times and are not reached then, they shall be considered in the order of the times to which they were postponed. It is not in order to postpone to a time beyond that session [§ 42] of the assembly, except* to the day of the next session, when it comes up with the unfinished business, and consequently takes precedence of new business [§ 44]. If it is desired to hold an adjourned meeting to consider a special subject, the time to which the assembly shall adjourn [§ 10] should be first fixed before making the motion to postpone the subject to that day.

22. To Commit [or Recommit, as it is called when the subject has been previously committed]. This motion takes precedence of the motions to Amend or Indefinitely Postpone, and yields to any Privileged [§ 9] or Incidental [§ 8] Question, and also to the motion to Lie on the Table, or for the Previous Question, or to Postpone to a certain day. It can be amended by altering the committee, or giving it instructions. It is debatable, and opens to debate [§ 35] the merits of the question it is proposed to commit.

The *Form* of this motion is, "to refer the subject to a committee." When different com-

---

*In Congress a motion cannot be postponed to the next session, but it is customary in ordinary societies.

mittees are proposed they should be voted on
in the following order: (1) Committee of
the whole [§ 32], (2) a standing committee,
and (3) a special (or select) committee. The
number of a committee is usually decided
without the formality of a motion, as in filling
blanks [§ 25]: the Chairman asks "Of how
many shall the committee consist?" and a
question is then put upon each number suggested, beginning with the largest. The number and kind of the committee need not be
decided till after it has been voted to refer the
subject to a committee.

If the committee is a select one, and the
motion does not include the method of appointing it, and there is no standing rule on
the subject, the Chairman inquires how the
committee shall be appointed, and this is usually decided informally. Sometimes the Chair
"appoints," in which case he names the members of the committee and no vote is taken
upon them; or the committee is "nominated"
either by the Chair or members of the assembly (no member nominating more than one except by general consent), and then they are all
voted upon together, except where more nominations are made than the number of the committee, when they shall be voted upon singly.

Where a committee is one for action (a committee of arrangements for holding a public meeting, for example), it should generally be small, and no one placed upon it who is not favorable to the proposed action; and if any such should be appointed, he should ask to be excused. But when the committee is for deliberation or investigation. it is of the utmost importance that all parties be represented on it, so that in committee the fullest discussion may take place, and thus diminish the chances of unpleasant debates in the assembly.

In ordinary assemblies, by judicious appointment of committees, debates upon delicate and troublesome questions can be mostly confined to the committees, which will contain the representative members of all parties. [See Committees, § 28.]

23. To Amend. This motion takes precedence of nothing but the question which it is proposed to amend, and yields to any Privileged [§ 9], Incidental [§ 8], or Subsidiary [§ 7] Question, except to Indefinitely Postpone. It can be amended itself, but this " amendment of an amendment " cannot be amended.

An Amendment may be inconsistent with one already adopted, or may directly conflict with the spirit of the original motion, but it must have a direct bearing upon the subject of that motion. *To illustrate:* a motion for a vote of thanks could be amended by substituting for " thanks " the word " censure ; " or one condemning certain customs could be amended by adding other customs.

An Amendment may be in any of the following forms : (*a*) to " *add* " or " *insert* " certain words or paragraphs ; (*b*) to " *strike out* " certain words or paragraphs, the question, however, being stated by the Chair thus : " Shall these words [or paragraphs] stand as a part of the resolution ? " * and if this is adopted, (that is, the motion to " strike out " fails,) it does not preclude either amendment or a motion to " strike out and insert ; " (*c*) " *to strike out certain words and insert others,*" which motion is indivisible, and if lost does not preclude another motion to strike out the same words and insert different ones ; (*d*) to " *substitute* " another motion on the same subject for the one pending ; (*e*) to " *divide the question* " into two or more questions as the mover specifies, so as to get a

---

* Whether the motion is to adopt or to strike out a paragraph, the principle is the same, the paragraph cannot stand as a part of the resolution unless a majority are in favor of it.

separate vote on any particular point or points [see § 4].

If a paragraph is inserted it should be perfected by its friends previous to voting on it, as when once inserted it cannot be struck out or amended except by adding to it. The same is true in regard to words to be inserted in a resolution, as when once inserted they cannot be struck out, except by a motion to strike out the paragraph, or such a portion of it as shall make the question an entirely different one from that of inserting the particular words. The principle involved is, that when the assembly has voted that certain words shall form a part of a resolution, it is not in order to make another motion which involves exactly the same question as the one they have decided. The only way to bring it up again is to move a Reconsideration [§ 27] of the vote by which the words were inserted.

The numbers prefixed to paragraphs are only marginal indications, and should be corrected, if necessary, by the clerk, without any motion to amend.

An Amendment to Rules of Order, By-Laws or a Constitution shall require previous notice, and a two-thirds vote for its adoption [see § 45].

[For amending reports of Committees and propositions containing several paragraphs, see § 44; for the proper form of stating the question on an amendment, see § 65.]

The following motions *cannot be amended*:

To Adjourn (when unqualified).........See § 11
For the Orders of the Day............ " § 13
All Incidental Questions .... " § 8
To Lie on the Table................. " § 19
For the Previous Question............ " § 20
An Amendment of an Amendment ..... " § 23
To Postpone Indefinitely .... " § 24
To Reconsider............ .. .. " § 27

24. To Postpone Indefinitely. This motion takes precedence of nothing except the Principal Question [§ 6], and yields to any Privileged [§ 9], Incidental [§ 8] or Subsidiary [§ 7] Motion, except to Amend. It cannot be amended; it opens to debate the entire question which it is proposed to postpone. Its effect is to entirely remove the question from before the assembly for that session [§ 42]. The Previous Question [§ 20], if ordered when this motion is pending, applies **only** to it without affecting the main question.

Miscellaneous Motions.

[§§ 25–27.]

25. Filling Blanks. In filling blanks the largest sum and the longest time proposed shall be first put to the question. Sometimes the most convenient way of amending a resolution is to create a blank by moving to strike out a certain number or time. It is customary for any number of members to propose numbers to fill a blank without the formality of a motion, these different propositions not being regarded in the light of amendments.

Nominations are treated in a similar manner, so that the second nomination, instead of being an amendment to the first, is an independent motion, which, if the first fails, is to be immediately voted upon. Any number of nominations can be made, the Chairman announcing each name as he hears it, and they should be voted upon in the order announced, until one receives a vote sufficient for an election.

26. Renewal of a Motion. When any Principal Question [§ 6] or Amendment has been once acted upon by the assembly, it cannot be taken up again at the same session

[§ 42] except by a motion to Reconsider
[§ 27]. The motion to Adjourn [§ 11] can
be renewed if there has been progress in debate, or any business transacted. As a general rule the introduction of any motion that
alters the state of affairs makes it admissible
to renew any Privileged or Incidental Motion,
(excepting a motion for the Orders of the Day
or for the Suspension of the Rules as provided in §§ 13, 18,) or Subsidiary Motion (excepting an Amendment), as in such a case the
real question before the assembly is a different one.

To illustrate : a motion that a question lie
on the table having failed, suppose afterwards
it be moved to refer the matter to a committee, it is now in order to move again that the
subject lie on the table; but such a motion
would not be in order if it were not made till
after the failure of the motion to commit, as
the question then resumes its previous condition.

When a subject has been referred to a
committee which reports at the same meeting,
the matter stands before the assembly as if
it had been introduced for the first time. A
motion which has been withdrawn has not

been acted upon, and therefore can be renewed.

27. Reconsider. It is in order at any time, even when another member has the floor, or while the assembly is voting on the motion to Adjourn, during the day* on which a motion has been acted upon, to move to "Reconsider the vote" and have such motion "entered on the record," but it cannot be considered while another question is before the assembly. It must be made, excepting when the vote is by ballot, by a member who voted with the prevailing side; for instance, in case a motion fails to pass for lack of a two-thirds vote, a reconsideration must be moved by one who voted against the motion.

A motion to reconsider the vote on a Subsidiary [§ 7] Motion takes precedence of the main question. It yields to Privileged [§ 9] Questions (except for the Orders of the Day) and Incidental [§ 8] Questions.

This motion can be *applied*† to the vote on

---

* In Congress any one can move a reconsideration, excepting where the vote is taken by yeas and nays [§ 38], when the rule above applies. The motion can be made on the same or succeeding day.

† It is not the practice to reconsider an affirmative vote on the motion to lie on the table, as the same result can be reached by

every other question, except to Adjourn and
to Suspend the Rules, and an affirmative vote
on to Lie on the Table or to Take from the
Table [§ 19]. No question can be twice
reconsidered. This motion cannot be amended; it is debatable or not, just as the question
to be reconsidered is debatable or undebatable
[§ 35]; when debatable, it opens up for discussion the entire subject to be reconsidered,
and the Previous Question [§ 20], if ordered
while it is pending, affects only the motion to
reconsider. It can be laid on the table [§ 19],
and in such cases the last motion cannot be
reconsidered; it is quite common and allowable to combine these two motions (though
they must be voted on separately). In this
case, the reconsideration, like any other
question, can be taken from the table, but
possesses no privilege.* The motion to reconsider being laid on the table does not carry
with it the pending measure. If an amend-

---

the motion to take from the table. For a similar reason, an
affirmative vote on a motion to take from the table cannot be
reconsidered.

* In Congress this is a common method used by the friends of
a measure to prevent its reconsideration, and is deemed a finality.
In ordinary societies it can be used safely only under the circumstances described in § 59 (c).

ment to a motion has been either adopted or
rejected, and then a vote taken on the motion
as amended, it is not in order to reconsider
the vote on the amendment until after the
vote on the original motion has been reconsidered. If the Previous Question [§ 20]
has been partly executed, it cannot be reconsidered. If anything which the assembly
cannot reverse has been done as the result of
a vote, then that vote cannot be reconsidered.

The *Effect of making* this motion is to
suspend all action that the original motion
would have required until the reconsideration
is acted upon; but if it is not called up, its
effect terminates with the session [§ 42], provided,* that in an assembly having regular
meetings as often as monthly, if there is not
held upon another day an adjourned meeting
of the one at which the reconsideration was
moved, its effect shall not terminate till the
close of the next succeeding session [see
note at end of this section]. But the reconsideration of an Incidental [§ 8] or Subsidiary
[§ 7] Motion (except where the vote to be re-

---

* In Congress the effect always terminates with the session,
and it cannot be called up by any one but the mover, until the
expiration of the time during which it is in order to move a
reconsideration.

considered had the effect to remove the whole
subject from before the assembly) shall be
immediately acted upon, as otherwise it would
prevent action on the main question.*

While this motion is so highly privileged as
far as relates to having it entered on the minutes, yet the reconsideration of another question cannot be made to interfere with the discussion of a question before the assembly, but
as soon as that subject is disposed of, the reconsideration, if called up, takes precedence
of everything except the motions to adjourn,
and to fix the time to which to adjourn.   As
long as its effect lasts (as shown above), any
one can call up the motion to reconsider, and
have it acted upon — excepting that when its
effect extends beyond the meeting at which

---

* Thus, suppose the motion to Indefinitely Postpone is negatived, showing that the assembly wish to consider the subject: if
it is moved to reconsider the last vote, then the reconsideration
must be immediately acted upon, as otherwise the whole subject
would be removed from before the assembly as shown above,
without any possible benefit to the assembly.   If the object is to
prevent a temporary majority from adopting a resolution, the
proper course is to wait until the resolution is finally acted upon,
and then move the reconsideration.   If the motion to Indefinitely
Postpone is carried, the subject is removed from before the
assembly, and consequently there is no hinderance to business in
permitting the reconsideration to hold over to another day.

the motion was made, no one but the mover can call it up at that meeting.

The *Effect of the adoption* of this motion is to place before the assembly the original question in the exact position it occupied before it was voted upon; consequently no one can debate the question reconsidered who had previously exhausted his right of debate [§ 34] on that question; his only resource is to discuss the question while the motion to reconsider is before the assembly. When a vote taken under the operation of the previous question is reconsidered, the question is then divested of the previous question, and is open to debate and amendment, provided the previous question had been exhausted [see § 20] by votes taken on all the questions covered by it, before the motion to reconsider was made.

A reconsideration requires only a majority vote, regardless of the vote necessary to adopt the motion reconsidered. [For reconsidering in committee see § 28.]

NOTE ON RECONSIDER.— In the English Parliament a vote once taken cannot be reconsidered, but in our Congress it is allowed to move a reconsideration of the vote on the same or succeeding day, and after the close of the last day for making the motion, any one can call up the motion to reconsider, so that this motion cannot delay action more than two days, and the effect of the motion, if not acted upon, terminates with the session. There seems to be no reason or good precedent for permitting merely two persons, by moving a reconsideration, to suspend for any length of time all action under resolutions adopted by the assembly, and yet where the delay is very short the advantages of reconsideration overbalance the evils.

Where a permanent society has meetings weekly or monthly, and usually only a small proportion of the society is present, it seems best to allow a reconsideration to hold over to another meeting, so that the society may have notice of what action is about to be taken. To prevent the motion being used to defeat a measure that cannot be deferred till the next regular meeting, it is provided that in case the society adjourn, to meet on a different day, then the reconsideration will not hold over beyond that session; this allows sufficient delay to notify the society, while, if the question is one requiring immediate action, the delay cannot extend beyond the day to which they adjourn. The rule provides that the adjourned meeting must be held on another day, in order to prevent the whole object of the reconsideration being defeated by an immediate adjournment to meet again in a few minutes. Where the meetings are only quarterly or annual the society should be properly represented at each meeting, and their best interests are subserved by following the practice of Congress, and letting the effect of the reconsideration terminate with the session.

Art. IV. Committees and Informal Action.

[§§ 28–33.]

28. Committees. It is usual in deliberative assemblies, to have all preliminary work in the preparation of matter for their action done by means of committees. These may be either "standing committees" (which are appointed for the session [§ 42], or for some definite time, as one year); or "select committees," appointed for a special purpose: or a "committee of the whole" [§ 32], consisting of the entire assembly. [For method of appointing committees of the whole, see § 32; other committees, see Commit, § 22.] The first person named on a committee is chairman (in his absence the next named member becomes chairman, and so on), and should act as such, unless the committee, by a majority of their number, elect another chairman, which they are competent to do. The clerk should furnish him, or some other member of the committee, with notice of the appointment of the committee, giving the names of the members, the matter referred to them, and such instructions as the assembly have decided upon. The chairman shall call the committee together, and, if there is a quorum (a majority of the committee, see § 43), he should read, or have read, the entire resolutions referred to them; he should then read each paragraph, and pause for amendments to be offered; when the amendments to that paragraph are voted on he proceeds to the next, only taking votes on amendments, as the committee cannot vote on the adoption of matter referred to them by the assembly.

If the committee originate the resolutions, they vote, in the same way, on amendments to each paragraph of the draft of the resolutions (which draft has been previously prepared by one of their members or a sub-committee); they do not vote on the separate paragraphs, but, having completed the amendments, they vote on the adoption of the entire report [see § 44]. When there is a preamble it is considered last. If the report originates with the committee, all amendments are to be incorporated in the report; but if the resolutions were referred, the committee cannot alter the text, but must submit the original paper intact, with their amendments (which may be in the form of a substitute, § 23) written on a separate sheet.

A committee is a miniature assembly that must meet together in order to transact business, and usually one of its members should be appointed its clerk. Whatever is not agreed to by the majority of the members present at a meeting (at which a quorum, consisting of a majority of the members of the committee, shall be present) cannot form a part of its report. The minority may be permitted to submit their views in writing also, either together, or each member separately, but their reports can only be acted upon by voting to substitute one of them for the report of the committee [see § 30]. The rules of the assembly, as far as possible, shall apply in committee; but a reconsideration [§ 27] of a vote shall be allowed, regardless of the time elapsed, only when every member who voted with the majority is present when the reconsideration is moved.* A committee (except a committee of the whole, § 32) may appoint a

---

* Both the English common parliamentary law and the rules of Congress prohibit the reconsideration of a vote by a committee ; but the strict enforcement of this rule in ordinary committees would interfere with rather than assist the transaction of business. The rule given above seems more just, and more in

sub-committee. When through with the business assigned them, a motion is made for the committee to "rise" (which is equivalent to the motion to adjourn), and that the chairman (or some member who is more familiar with the subject) make its report to the assembly. The committee ceases to exist as soon as the assembly receives the report [§ 30].

The committee has no power to punish its members for disorderly conduct, its resource being to report the facts to the assembly. No allusion can be made in the assembly to what has occurred in committee, except it be by a report of the committee, or by general consent. It is the duty of a committee to meet on the call of any two of its members, if the Chairman be absent or decline to appoint such meeting. When a committee adjourns without appointing a time for the next meeting, it is called together in the same way as at its first meeting. When a committee adjourns to meet at another time, it is not necessary (though usually advisable) that absent members should be notified of the adjourned meeting.

---

accordance with the practice of ordinary committees, who usually reconsider at pleasure. No improper advantage can be taken of the privilege, as long as every member who voted with the majority must be present when the reconsideration is moved.

29. Forms of Reports of Committees. The form of a report is usually similar to the following:

A standing committee reports thus: "The committee on [insert name of committee] respectfully report," [or "beg leave to report," or "beg leave to submit the following report,"] etc., letting the report follow.

A select or special committee reports as follows: "The committee to which was referred [state the matter referred] having considered the same, respectfully report," etc. Or for "The committee" is sometimes written "Your committee," or "The undersigned, a committee."

When a minority report is submitted, it should be in this form (the majority reporting as above): "The undersigned, a minority of a committee to which was referred," etc. The majority report is the report of the committee, and should never be made out as the report of the majority.

All reports conclude with, "All of which is respectfully submitted." They are sometimes signed only by the chairman of the committee, but if the matter is of much importance, it is better that the report be signed by every mem-

ber who concurs.   The report is not usually
dated or addressed, but can be headed, as, for
example, "Report of the Finance Committee
of the Y. P. A., on Renting a Hall."   The
report of a committee should generally close
or be accompanied with formal resolutions
covering all their recommendations, so that the
adopting of their report [§ 31] would have the
effect to adopt all the resolutions necessary to
carry out their recommendations.*

30. Reception of Reports. When the
report of a committee is to be made, the Chairman (or member appointed to make the report)
informs the assembly that the committee to
whom was referred such a subject or paper,
has directed him to make a report thereon, or
report it with or without amendment, as the
case may be; either he or any other member
may move that it be "received" † now or at
some other specified time.

---

* If the report of a committee were written in this form, "Your
committee think the conduct of Mr. A at the last meeting so dis-
graceful that they would recommend that he be expelled from the
society," the adoption of the report would not have the effect to
expel the member.

† A very common error is, after a report has been read, to
move that it be received ; whereas the fact that it has been read
shows that it has been already received by the assembly.
Another mistake, less common, but dangerous, is to vote that the

Usually the formality of a vote on the reception of a report of a committee is dispensed with, the time being settled by general consent. Should any one object, a formal motion becomes necessary. When the time arrives for the assembly to receive the report, the chairman of the committee reads it in his place and then delivers it to the clerk, when it lies on the table till the assembly sees fit to consider it. If the report consists of a paper with amendments, the chairman of the committee reads the amendments with the coherence in the paper, explaining the alterations and the reasons of the committee for the amendments, till he has gone through the whole. If the report is very long it is not usually read until the assembly is ready to consider it [see §§ 31, 44].

When the report has been received, whether it has been read or not, the committee is thereby dissolved, and can act no more unless it is

report be accepted (which is equivalent to adopting it, see § 31) when the intention is only to have the report up for consideration and afterwards move its adoption. Still a third error is, to move that "the report be adopted and the committee be discharged," when the committee have reported in full and their report has been received, so that the committee have already ceased to exist. If the committee, however, have made but a partial report, or report progress, then it is in order to move that the committee be discharged from the further consideration of the subject.

revived by a vote to recommit.   If the report is recommitted, all the parts of the report that have not been agreed to by the assembly are ignored by the committee as if the report had never been made.

If any member or members wish to submit a minority report (or reports) it is customary to receive it immediately after receiving the report of the committee; but it cannot be acted upon unless a motion is made to substitute it for the report of the committee.

31. Adoption of Reports. When the assembly is to consider a report, a motion should be made to "adopt," "accept," or "agree to" the report, all of which, when carried, have the same effect, namely, to make the doings of the committee become the acts of the assembly, the same as if done by the assembly without the intervention of a committee.   While these motions are generally used indiscriminately, and all have the same effect, still it would probably be better to vary the motion according to the character of the report.   Thus if the report contains merely a statement of opinion or facts, the best form of the motion is to "accept the report;" if it also concludes with resolutions or orders, the motion would

be more appropriately "to agree to the resolutions," or "to adopt the orders." *   If either
of these latter motions is carried, the effect is
to adopt the entire report of the committee.

After either of the above motions is made,
the report is open to amendment, and the
matter stands before the assembly exactly the
same as if there had been no committee, and
the subject had been introduced by the motion of the member who made the report.
[See § 34 for his privileges in debate, and
§ 44 for the method of treating a report containing several propositions, when being considered by the assembly.]

32. Committee of the Whole. When
an assembly has to consider a subject which it
does not wish to refer to a committee, and yet
where the subject-matter is not well digested
and put into proper form for its definite action, or when, for any other reason, it is desirable for the assembly to consider a subject

---

* "To adopt" the report is the most common of these motions in ordinary societies, and is used regardless of the character of the report.   Its effect is generally understood, which is
not the case with the motion to accept, as shown in the note to
§ 30 [which see for common errors in acting upon reports].   The
last paragraph of § 29 shows how the form of the report influ-
ences the effect of its adoption.

with all the freedom of an ordinary committee, it is the practice to refer the matter to the
"Committee of the Whole."* If it is desired to consider the question at once, the
motion is made, " That the assembly do now
resolve itself into a committee of the whole,
to take under consideration," etc., specifying
the subject. This is really a motion to " commit." [See § 22 for its order of precedence, etc.]
If adopted, the Chairman immediately calls
another member to the chair, and takes his
place as a member of the committee. The
committee is under the rules of the assembly,
excepting as stated hereafter in this section.

The only motions in order are to amend
and adopt, and that the committee " rise and
report," as it cannot adjourn; nor can it order
the "yeas and nays" [§ 38]. The only way
to close or limit debate in committee of the
whole is for the assembly to vote that the
debate in committee shall cease at a certain
time, or that after a certain time no debate
shall be allowed excepting on new amend-

---

* In large assemblies, such as the U. S. House of Representatives, where a member can speak to any question but once, the
committee of the whole seems almost a necessity, as it allows the
freest discussion of a subject, while at any time it can rise and
thus bring into force the strict rules of the assembly.

ments, and then only one speech in favor of
and one against it, of say five minutes each;
or in some other way regulate the time for
debate.*

If no limit is prescribed, any member may
speak as often as he can get the floor, and as
long each time as is allowed in debate in the
assembly, provided no one wishes the floor
who has not spoken on that particular question.　Debate having been closed at a particular time by order of the assembly, it is not
competent for the committee, even by unanimous consent, to extend the time.　The committee cannot refer the subject to another
committee.　Like other committees [§ 28], it
cannot alter the text of any resolution referred
to it; but if the resolution originated in the
committee, then all the amendments are incorporated in it.

---

* In Congress no motion to limit debate in committee of the
whole is in order till after the subject has been already considered
in committee of the whole.　As no subject would probably be
considered more than once in committee of the whole, in an ordinary society, the enforcement of this rule would practically
prevent such a society from putting any limit to debate in the
committee.　The rule, as given above, allows the society, whenever resolving itself into committee of the whole, to impose upon
the debate in the committee such restrictions as are allowed in
Congress after the subject has already been considered in committee of the whole.

When it is through with the consideration
of the subject referred to it, or if it wishes to
adjourn, or to have the assembly limit debate,
a motion is made that "the committee rise
and report," etc., specifying the result of its
proceedings.   This motion "to rise" is equivalent to the motion to adjourn in the assembly, and is always in order (except when
another member has the floor), and is undebatable.   As soon as this motion is adopted
the presiding officer takes the chair, and the
chairman of the committee, having resumed
his place in the assembly, rises and informs
him that "the committee have gone through
the business referred to them, and that he is
ready to make the report when the assembly
is ready to receive it;" or he will make such
other report as will suit the case.

The clerk does not record the proceedings
of the committee on the minutes, but should
keep a memorandum of the proceedings for
the use of the committee.   In large assemblies the clerk vacates his chair, which is
occupied by the chairman of the committee,
and the assistant clerk acts as clerk of the
committee.   Should the committee get disorderly, and the chairman be unable to preserve

order, the presiding officer can take the chair, and declare the committee dissolved. The quorum of the committee of the whole is the same as that of the assembly [§ 43]. If the committee finds itself without a quorum, it can only rise and report the fact to the assembly, which in such a case would have to adjourn.

33. Informal Consideration of a Question (or acting as if in committee of the whole).

It has become customary in many assemblies, instead of going into committee of the whole, to consider the question "informally," and afterwards to act "formally." In a small assembly there is no objection to this.* While acting informally upon any resolutions, the assembly can only amend and adopt them, and without further motion the Chairman announces that "the assembly, acting informally, [or as in committee of the whole,] has had such subject under consideration, and has

---

* In the U. S. Senate all bills, joint resolutions and treaties, upon their second reading are considered "as if the Senate were in committee of the whole," which is equivalent to considering them informally. [U. S. Senate Rules, 28 and 38.] In large assemblies it is better to follow the practice of the House of Representatives, and go into committee of the whole.

made certain amendments, which he will report." The subject comes before the assembly then as if reported by a committee. While acting informally the Chairman retains his seat, as it is not necessary to move that the committee rise; but at any time the adoption of such motions as to adjourn, the previous question, to commit, or any motion except to amend or adopt, puts an end to the informal consideration; as, for example, the motion to commit is equivalent to the following motions when in committee of the whole: (1) That the committee rise; (2) that the committee of the whole be discharged from the further consideration of the subject, and (3) that it be referred to a committee.

While acting informally every member can speak as many times as he pleases, and as long each time as permitted in the assembly [§ 34], and the informal action may be rejected or altered by the assembly. While the clerk should keep a memorandum of the informal proceedings, it should not be entered on the minutes, being only for temporary use. The Chairman's report to the assembly of the informal action should be entered on the

6

minutes, as it belongs to the assembly's proceedings.

Art. V.   Debate and Decorum.
[§§ 34-37.]

34. Debate.* When a motion is made and
seconded, it shall be stated by the Chairman
before being debated [see § 3]. When any
member is about to speak in debate he shall
rise and respectfully address himself to "Mr.
Chairman." ["Mr. President" is used where
that is the designated title of the presiding
officer; "Mr. Moderator"† is more common
in religious meetings. In every case the
presiding officer should be addressed by his
official title.] The Chairman shall then announce his name [see § 2]. By parliamentary
courtesy, the member upon whose motion a
subject is brought before the assembly is first

---

* In connection with this section read §§ 1-5.

† "Brother Moderator" is more commonly used in some sections of the country; but in strictness of speech it implies an
official equality between the speaker and the Chairman that does
not exist, or in other words it implies that they are both mod-
erators. If a woman is in the chair, the only change in the
address is by substituting "Mrs." or "Miss," as the case may
be, for "Mr." Thus, "Mrs. President."

entitled to the floor, even though another member has risen first and addressed the Chair [in case of a report of a committee, it is the member who presents the report]; and this member is also entitled to close the debate, but not until every member choosing to speak has spoken. When a member reports a measure from a committee, he cannot in any way be deprived of his right to close the debate; so if the previous question [§ 20] is ordered the Chairman at once assigns him the floor to close the debate. With this exception, no member shall speak more than twice to the same question (only once to a question of order, § 14), nor longer than ten minutes at one time, without leave of the assembly, and the question upon granting the leave shall be decided by a majority vote without debate.* If greater freedom is desired, the proper course

---

* The limit in time should vary to suit circumstances, but the limit of two speeches of ten minutes each will usually answer in ordinary assemblies, and it can be increased, when desirable, by a majority vote as shown above, or diminished as shown in § 37. In the U. S. House of Representatives no member can speak more than once to the same question, nor longer than one hour. The fourth rule of the Senate is as follows: "No senator shall speak more than twice in any one debate, on the same day, without leave of the Senate, which question shall be decided without debate." If no rule is adopted, each member can speak but once to the same question.

is to refer the subject to the committee of the whole [§ 32], or to consider it informally [§ 33]. [For limiting or closing the debate see § 37.]

No member can speak the second time to a question until every member choosing to speak has spoken. But an amendment, or any other motion, being offered, makes the real question before the assembly a different one, and, in regard to the right to debate, is treated as a new question. Merely asking a question, or making a suggestion, is not considered as speaking. The maker of a motion, though he can vote against it, cannot speak against his own motion.

35. Undebatable Questions and those Opening the Main Question to Debate.

The following questions shall be decided without debate, all others being debatable [see note at end of this section]:

To *Fix the Time to which the Assembly shall Adjourn* (when a privileged question, § 10).

To *Adjourn* [§ 11] (or in committee, *to rise*, which is used instead of to adjourn).

For the *Orders of the Day* [§ 13], and questions relating to the *priority of business*.

An *Appeal* [§ 14], when made while the Previous Question is pending, or when simply relating to indecorum or transgressions of the rules of speaking, or to the priority of business.

Objection to the Consideration of a Question [§ 15].

To *Lie on the Table*, or to *Take from the Table* [§ 19].

The *Previous Question* [§ 20].

To *Reconsider* [§ 27] a question which is itself undebatable.

Questions relating to *Reading of Papers* [§ 16], or *Withdrawing a Motion* [§ 17], or *Suspending the Rules* [§ 18], or *extending the limits of debate* [§ 34], or *limiting or closing debate* [§ 37], or granting *leave to continue his speech* to one who has been guilty of indecorum in debate [§ 36].

The motion *to postpone to a certain time*, [§ 21] allows of but very limited debate, which must be confined to the propriety of the postponement. When an *amendment* is before the assembly the main question cannot be debated excepting so far as it is necessarily involved in the amendment. But the following motions open to discussion the entire merits of the main question :

To Commit [§ 22].

To Postpone Indefinitely [§ 24].

To Reconsider a debatable question [§ 27].

The distinction between debate and making suggestions or asking a question should always be kept in view, and, when the latter will assist the assembly in determining the question, is allowed, to a limited extent, even though the question before the assembly is undebatable.

NOTE ON UNDEBATABLE QUESTIONS.—The English common parliamentary law makes all motions debatable, unless there is a rule adopted limiting debate [Cushing's Manual, § 330]; but every assembly is obliged to restrict debate upon certain motions. The restrictions to debate prescribed in this section conform to the practice of Congress, where, however, it is very common to allow of brief remarks upon the most undebatable questions, sometimes five or six members speaking. This, of course, is allowed only when no one objects.

By examining the above list it will be found that, while free debate is allowed upon every principal question [§ 6], it is permitted or prohibited upon other questions in accordance with the following principles:

(*a*) Highly privileged questions, as a rule, should not be debated, as in that case they could be used to prevent the assembly from coming to a vote on the main question (for instance, if the motion to adjourn were debatable, it could be used [see § 11] in a way to greatly hinder business). *High privilege is, as a rule, incompatible with the right of debate on the privileged question.*

(*b*) A motion that has the effect to suppress a question before the assembly, so that it cannot again be taken up that session [§ 42], allows of free debate; and a Subsidiary Motion [§7, except Commit, which see below,] is debatable to just the extent that it interferes with the right of the assembly to take up the original question at its pleasure.

Illustrations: To " Indefinitely Postpone " [§ 24] a question places it out of the power of the assembly to again take it up during that session, and consequently this motion allows of free debate, even, involving the whole merits of the original question.

To "Postpone to a certain time" prevents the assembly taking up the question till the specified time, and therefore allows of limited debate upon the propriety of the postponement.

To "Lie on the Table" leaves the question so that the assembly can at any time consider it, and therefore should not be, and is not debatable.

To "Commit" would not be very debatable, according to this rule, but it is an exception, because it is often important that the committee should know the views of the assembly on the question, and it therefore is not only debatable, but opens to debate the whole question which it is proposed to refer to the committee.

36. Decorum in Debate [see § 2].　In debate a member must confine himself to the question before the assembly, and avoid personalities.　He cannot reflect upon any act of the assembly, unless he intends to conclude his remarks with a motion to rescind such action, or else while debating such motion.　In referring to another member, he should, as much as possible, avoid using his name, rather referring to him as "the member who spoke last," or in some other way describing him. The officers of the assembly should always be referred to by their official titles.　It is not allowable to arraign the motives of a member, but the nature or consequences of a measure

may be condemned in strong terms. It is not
the man, but the measure, that is the subject
of debate. If at any time the Chairman rises
to state a point of order, or give information,
or otherwise speak, within his privilege [see
§ 40], the member speaking must take his seat
till the Chairman has been first heard. When
called to order, the member must sit down
until the question of order is decided. If his
remarks are decided to be improper, he cannot
proceed, if any one objects, without the leave
of the assembly expressed by a vote, upon
which question there shall be no debate.

Disorderly words should be taken down by
the member who objects to them, or by the
clerk, and then read to the member; if he
denies them, the assembly shall decide by a
vote whether they are his words or not. If a
member cannot justify the words he used, and
will not suitably apologize for using them, it is
the duty of the assembly to act in the case.
If the disorderly words are of a personal
nature, before the assembly proceeds to deliberate upon the case both parties to the per-
sonality should retire, it being a general rule
that no member should be present in the assembly when any matter relating to himself is

under debate. It is not, however, necessary for the member objecting to the words to retire, unless he is personally involved in the case. If any business has taken place since the member spoke, it is too late to take notice of any disorderly words he used.

During debate, and while the Chairman is speaking, or the assembly is engaged in voting, no member is permitted to disturb the assembly by whispering, or walking across the floor, or in any other way.

37. Closing Debate. Debate upon a question is not closed by the Chairman rising to put the question, as, until both the affirmative and negative are put, a member can claim the floor, and reopen debate [see § 38]. Debate can be closed by the following motions,* which are undebatable [§ 35], and, except to Lie on the Table, shall require a two-thirds † vote for their adoption [§ 39]:

---

* It will be noticed that the first two of these motions only close debate by virtue of their suppressing the question itself. The circumstances under which each of these motions to suppress debate and to suppress the question should be used, are explained in §§ 58, 59.

† In Congress, where each speaker can occupy the floor one hour, any of these motions to cut off debate can be adopted by a mere majority. In ordinary societies harmony is so essential that a two-thirds vote should be required to force the assembly to a final vote without allowing free debate [see note to § 39].

(*a*) *An Objection to the Consideration of a Question* [only allowable when the question is first introduced, § 15], which, if sustained, not only stops debate, but also throws the subject out of the assembly for that session [§ 42]; which latter effect is the one for which it was designed.

(*b*) To *Lie on the Table* [§ 19], which, if adopted, carries the question to the table, from which it cannot be taken unless a majority favor such action.

(*c*) The *Previous Question* [§ 20], which, if adopted, cuts off debate, and brings the assembly to a vote on the pending question only, excepting where the pending motion is an amendment or a motion to commit, when it also applies to the question to be amended or committed. It may be applied merely to an amendment, or to an amendment of an amendment.

(*d*) For the assembly to adopt an *order* (1) *limiting debate* upon a special subject, either as to the number or length of the speeches; or (2) *closing debate* upon the subject at a stated time, when all pending questions shall be put to vote without further debate. Either of these two measures may be applied simply to a pending amendment, or an amendment thereto; and when this is voted upon, the original question is still open to debate and amendment.

Art. VI. Vote.

[§§ 38, 39.]

38. Voting. Whenever from the nature of the question it permits of no modification or debate, the Chairman immediately puts it to vote; if the question is debatable, when the Chairman thinks the debate has been brought to a close he should inquire if the assembly is ready for the question, and if no one rises he puts the question to vote. There are various forms for putting the question in use in different parts of the country. The rule in Congress, in the House of Representatives, is as follows: "Questions shall be distinctly put in this form, to wit: 'As many as are of the opinion that [as the question may be] say *Aye;*' and after the affirmative voice is expressed, 'As many as are of the contrary opinion, say *No.*'" The following form is

very common: "It has been moved and seconded that [here state the question]. As
many as are in favor of the motion say *Aye;*
those opposed *No.*" Or, if the motion is for
the adoption of a certain resolution, after it
has been read the Chairman can say, "You
have heard the resolution read; those in favor
of its adoption will hold up the right hand;
those opposed will manifest it by the same
sign." These examples * are sufficient to
show the usual methods of putting a question,
the affirmative being always put first.

When a vote is taken the Chairman should
always announce the result in the following
form: "The motion is carried — the resolution is adopted," or, "The ayes have it — the
resolution is adopted." If, when he announces
a vote, any member rises and states that he
doubts the vote, or calls for a "division," the
Chairman shall say, "A division is called for;
those in favor of the motion will rise." After
counting these, and announcing the number,
he shall say, "Those opposed will rise." He
will count these, announce the number, and
declare the result; that is, whether the motion

---

* See § 65 and also the Table of Rules, p. 10, for the forms of
stating and putting certain questions.

is carried or lost. Instead of counting the vote himself, he can appoint tellers to make the count and report to him. When tellers are appointed, they should be selected from both sides of the question. A member has the right to change his vote (when not made by ballot) before the decision of the question has been finally and conclusively pronounced by the Chair, but not afterwards.

Until the negative is put, it is in order for any member, in the same manner as if the voting had not been commenced, to rise and speak, make motions for amendment or otherwise, and thus renew the debate; and this, whether the member was in the assembly room or not when the question was put and the vote partly taken. After the Chairman has announced the vote, if it is found that a member had risen and addressed the Chair before the negative had been put, he is entitled to be heard on the question, the same as though the vote had not been taken. In such cases the question is in the same condition as if it had never been put.

No one can vote on a question affecting himself; but if more than one name is included in the resolution (though a sense of delicacy

would prevent this right being exercised, excepting when it would change the vote) all
are entitled to vote; for if this were not so, a
minority could control an assembly by including the names of a sufficient number in a
motion, say for preferring charges against
them, and suspend them, or even expel them
from the assembly.*

When there is a tie vote the motion fails,
unless the Chairman gives his vote for the
affirmative, which in such case he can do.
Where his vote will make a tie, he can cast it
and thus defeat the measure [§ 40]. However,
if there is a tie vote on the motion to "strike
out" [§ 23] the words are struck out, because
the question which has failed is, "Shall these
words stand as a part of the resolution?" But
in case of an Appeal [§ 14], though the question is, "Shall the decision of the Chair stand
as the judgment of the assembly"? a tie vote
sustains the Chair, upon the principle that the
decision of the Chair can only be reversed by
a majority.

Another form of voting is by *ballot*. This

---

* But, after charges are preferred against a member, and the
assembly has ordered him to appear for trial, he is theoretically
in arrest, and is deprived of all rights of membership until his
case is disposed of.

method is only adopted when required by the constitution or by-laws of the assembly, or when the assembly has ordered the vote to be so taken. The Chairman, in such cases, appoints at least two tellers, who distribute slips of paper, upon which each member, including the Chairman,* writes his vote. The votes are then collected, counted by the tellers, and the result reported to the Chairman, who announces it to the assembly. The Chairman announces the result of the vote, in case of an election to office, in a manner similar to the following: ' The whole number of votes cast is —; the number necessary for an election is —; Mr. A received —: Mr. B, —; Mr. C, —. Mr. B, having received the required number, is elected —." Where there is only one candidate for an office, and the constitution requires the vote to be by ballot, it is common to authorize the clerk to cast the vote of the assembly for such and such a person; if anyone objects, however, it is necessary to ballot in the usual way. So, when a motion is made to make a vote unanimous, it fails if anyone objects. In counting the ballots all blanks are ignored.

---

* Should the Chairman neglect to vote before the ballots are counted, he cannot then vote without the permission of the assembly.

The assembly can, by a majority vote, order that the vote on any question be taken by *Yeas and Nays.** In this method of voting the Chairman states both sides of the question at once; the clerk calls the roll, and each member, as his name is called, rises and answers *yes* or *no*, and the clerk notes his answer. Upon the completion of the roll-call the clerk reads over the names of those who answered in the affirmative, and afterwards those in the negative, that mistakes may be corrected; he then

---

* Taking a vote by yeas and nays, which has the effect to place on the record how each member votes, is peculiar to this country, and, while it consumes a great deal of time, is rarely useful in ordinary societies. While it can never be used to hinder business, as long as the above rule is observed, it should not be used at all in a mass meeting, or in any other assembly whose members are not responsible to a constituency. By the Constitution, one-fifth of the members present can, in either house of Congress, order a vote to be taken by yeas and nays, and, to avoid some of the resulting inconveniences, Congress has required, for instance, that the previous question shall be seconded by a majority, thus avoiding the yeas and nays until a majority are in favor of ordering the main question. In representative bodies this method of voting is very useful, especially where the proceedings are published, as it enables the people to know how their representatives voted on important measures. If there is no legal or constitutional provision for the yeas and nays being ordered by a minority in a representative body, they should adopt a rule allowing the yeas and nays to be ordered by a one-fifth vote, as in Congress, or even by a much smaller number. In some small bodies a vote on a resolution must be taken by yeas and nays, upon the demand of a single member.

gives the number voting on each side to the Chairman, who announces the result. An entry must be made in the minutes of the names of all voting in the affirmative, and also of those in the negative.

The form of putting a question upon which the vote has been ordered to be taken by yeas and nays is similar to the following: "As many as are in favor of the adoption of these resolutions will, when their names are called, answer *yes* [or *aye*]; those opposed will answer *no*." The Chairman will then direct the clerk to call the roll. The negative being put at the same time as the affirmative, it is too late, after the question is put, to renew the debate. After the commencement of the roll-call it is too late to ask to be excused from voting. The yeas and nays cannot be ordered in committee of the whole [§ 32].

39. Motions Requiring More than a Majority Vote. The following motions shall require a two-thirds vote for their adoption, all others requiring a majority, as the right of discussion, and the right to have the rules enforced, should not be abridged by a mere majority:

To Amend the Rules (requires previous
  notice also) .... See § 45
To Suspend the Rules .... " § 18
To Make a Special Order .... " § 13
*To Take up a Question out of its Proper
  Order* .... " § 13
*An Objection to the Consideration of a
  Question** .... " § 15
The Previous Question .... " § 20
To Close or Limit Debate .... " § 37

NOTE ON MOTIONS REQUIRING MORE THAN A
MAJORITY VOTE.— Every motion in this list has the
effect to suspend or change some rule or custom of
deliberative bodies. Judging from their form, this
would be true of only the first two, but a closer ex-
amination will show that the others have a similar
effect.

To take up a question out of its proper order, is a
change in the order of business.

An objection to the consideration of a question, if
sustained, suspends or conflicts with the right of a
member to introduce a measure to the assembly; a
right which certainly has been established by custom,
if it is not inherent to the very idea of a deliberative
body.   [Though Rule 41 H. R. allows a majority
vote to decide this question, it is so inexpedient that
the rule has not been taken advantage of lately.]

The *Previous Question*, and motions to *close or limit
debate*, have the effect of forcing the assembly to take
final action upon a question without allowing discussion; in other words, they suspend this fundamental
principle of deliberative bodies, namely, that the
assembly shall not be forced to final action on a

---

* The negative vote on considering the question must be two-
thirds to dismiss the question for that session.

question until every member has had an opportunity of discussing its merits.   The very idea of a deliberative assembly is that it is a body to deliberate upon questions, and therefore members must have the right of introducing questions, and of discussing their merits, before expressing their deliberate sense upon them.   [Of course a majority can lay the question on the table, and thus stop debate; but in this case the assembly can at any time take it from the table.   By this means the majority can instantly get rid of any question until they wish to consider it.]

But there are times when it is expedient to suspend these rights to introduce and debate questions, just the same as it is frequently an advantage to suspend the rules of the assembly, or to change the order of business.   If, however, a bare majority could at any time suspend or change these rules and privileges, they would be of but little value.   Experience has shown that a two-thirds vote should be required to adopt any motion that has the effect to suspend or change the rules or established order of business, and the rule above is made on this general principle. [The old parliamentary practice did not allow of a suspension of the rules except by unanimous consent.]

As just stated, Congress, by rule, allows a majority to sustain an objection to the consideration of a question, but the rule has very properly gone out of use.   So, too, the Previous Question, and motions to close or limit debate, while not used in the Senate, can be adopted by a majority in the House of Representatives.

On account of the immense amount of business to be transacted during each session by the National House of Representatives, and the large number of members each one of whom is entitled to the floor in debate for one hour, it seems an absolute necessity for them to permit a majority to limit or cut off entirely the debate, and thus practically to suspend one of the fundamental rules of deliberative bodies.   This is the more necessary in Congress because the party lines are strictly drawn, and the minority could almost stop legislation if they could prevent the debate from being cut off.

In all bodies situated in these respects like Congress, a rule should be adopted allowing a majority to adopt the previous question, and motions to limit or close debate. [See the last note to § 38 in reference to the yeas and nays being ordered by a one-fifth vote in Congress, and by even a smaller vote in some other bodies. The two notes in the Introduction, on pp. 15–17, may be read with advantage in connection with this note.]

Art. VII. The Officers and the Minutes.

[§§ 40, 41.]

40. Chairman* or President. The presiding officer, when no special title has been assigned him, is ordinarily called the Chairman (or in religious assemblies more usually the Moderator); frequently the constitution of the assembly prescribes for him a title, such as President.

His duties are generally as follows:

To open the session at the time at which the assembly is to meet, by taking the chair

---

* In connection with this section read §§ 2, 34, 44, 65.

and calling the members to order; to announce the business before the assembly in
the order in which it is to be acted upon
[§ 44]; to state and to put to vote [§§ 38, 65]
all questions which are regularly moved, or
necessarily arise in the course of proceedings,
and to announce the result of the vote;

To restrain the members, when engaged in
debate, within the rules of order; to enforce
on all occasions the observance of order and
decorum [§ 36] among the members, deciding
all questions of order (subject to an appeal to
the assembly by any two members, § 14), and
to inform the assembly when necessary, or
when referred to for the purpose, on a point
of order or practice;

To authenticate, by his signature, when
necessary, all the acts, orders and proceedings
of the assembly, and in general to represent
and stand for the assembly, declaring its will,
and in all things obeying its commands.

The Chairman shall rise * to put a question
to vote, but may state it sitting; he shall also
rise from his seat (without calling any one to
the chair) when speaking to a question of

---

* It is not customary for the Chairman to rise while putting
questions in very small bodies, such as committees, boards of
trustees, etc.

order, which he can do in preference to other
members.   In referring to himself he should
always use his official title, thus: "The Chair
decides so and so," not "I decide, etc."
When a member has the floor, the Chairman
cannot interrupt him so long as he does not
transgress any of the rules of the assembly,
excepting as provided in § 2.

He is entitled to vote when the vote is by
ballot,* and in all other cases where the vote
would change the result.   Thus, in a case
where a two-thirds vote is necessary, and his
vote thrown with the minority would prevent
the adoption of the question, he can cast his
vote; so, also, he can vote with the minority
when it will produce a tie vote and thus cause
the motion to fail.   Whenever a motion is
made referring especially to the Chairman, the
maker of the motion should put it to vote.

The Chairman can, if it is necessary to va-
cate the chair, appoint a Chairman *pro tem.,*†

---

* But this right is lost if he does not use it before the tellers
have commenced to count the ballots.   The assembly can give
leave to the Chairman to vote under such circumstances.

† When there are Vice-Presidents, then the first one on the
list that is present is, by virtue of his office, Chairman during the
absence of the President, and should always be called to the chair
when the President temporarily vacates it.

but the first adjournment puts an end to the appointment, which the assembly can terminate before, if it pleases, by electing another Chairman.   But the regular Chairman, knowing that he will be absent from a future meeting, cannot authorize another member to act in his place at such meeting; the clerk [§ 41], or, in his absence, any member should, in such case, call the meeting to order, and a Chairman *pro tem.* be elected, who would hold office during that session [§ 42], unless such office was terminated by the entrance of the regular Chairman.   If there are Vice-Presidents, the first on the list that is present takes the chair during the absence of the President.

The Chairman sometimes calls a member to the chair, and himself takes part in the debate; but this should rarely be done, and nothing can justify it in a case where much feeling is shown, and there is a liability to difficulty in preserving order.   If the Chairman has even the appearance of being a partisan, he loses much of his ability to control those who are on the opposite side of the question.*

---

* The unfortunate habit many chairmen have of constantly speaking on questions before the assembly, even interrupting the member who has the floor, is unjustified by either the common parliamentary law or the practice of Congress.   One who

The Chairman should not only be familiar with parliamentary usage, and set the example of strict conformity thereto,* but he should be a

---

expects to take an active part in debate should never accept the chair.

"It is a general rule in all deliberative assemblies, that the presiding officer shall not participate in the debate, or other proceedings, in any other capacity than as such officer. He is only allowed, therefore, to state matters of fact within his knowledge ; to inform the assembly on points of order or the course of proceeding, when called upon for that purpose, or when he finds it necessary to do so ; and, on appeals from his decision on questions of order, to address the assembly in debate." [Cushing's Manual, page 106.]

"Though the Speaker [Chairman] may of right speak to matters of order and be first heard, he is restrained from speaking on any other subject except where the assembly have occasion for facts within his knowledge ; then he may, with their leave, state the matter of fact." [Jefferson's Manual, sec. xvii, and Barclay's "Digest of the Rules and Practice of the House of Representatives U. S.," page 195.]

* No rules will take the place of tact and common sense on the part of the chairman. While usually he need not wait for motions of routine, or for a motion to be seconded when he knows it is favored by others [see first note to § 65], yet if this is objected to, it is safer instantly to require the forms of parliamentary law to be observed. By general consent many things can be done that will save much time, but where the assembly is divided and contains members who are continually raising points of order, the most expeditious and safe course is to enforce strictly all the rules and forms of parliamentary law.

Whenever an improper motion is made, instead of simply ruling it out of order, it is well for the Chairman to suggest how the desired object can be accomplished. Thus, if it is moved "to postpone the question," he should say that if the time is not specified the proper motion is "that the question lie on the table." So, if it were moved "to lay the question on the table until a certain time," he should suggest that the proper motion is "to postpone the question to that time."

man of executive ability, capable of controlling men; and it should never be forgotten, that, to control others, it is necessary to control one's self. An excited chairman can scarcely fail to cause trouble in a meeting.

A chairman will often find himself perplexed with the difficulties attending his position, and in such cases he will do well to heed the advice of a distinguished writer on parliamentary law, and recollect that

" The great purpose of all rules and forms is to subserve the will of the assembly rather than to restrain it ; to facilitate, and not to obstruct, the expression of their deliberate sense."

41. Clerk or Secretary [*and the Minutes*]. The recording officer is usually called the " Clerk " or " Secretary,"* and the record of proceedings the " Minutes." His desk should

---

* When there are two secretaries, he is termed the "recording secretary," and the other one the "corresponding secretary." In many societies the secretary, besides acting as recording officer, collects the dues of members, and thus becomes to a certain extent a financial officer. In most cases the treasurer acts as banker, only paying on the order of the society, signed by the secretary alone, or by the president and secretary. In such cases the secretary becomes in reality the financial officer of the society, and should make reports to the society of funds received and from what sources, and of the funds expended and for what purposes. See § 52 for his duties as financial officer.

be near that of the Chairman, and in the absence of the Chairman (if there is no vice-president present), when the hour for opening the session arrives, it is his duty to call the meeting to order, and to preside until the election of a chairman *pro tem.*, which should be done immediately. He should keep a record of the proceedings, commencing in a form similar to the following:* "At a regular quarterly meeting of [state the name of the society], held on the 31st day of March, 1875, at [state the place of meeting], the President in the chair, the minutes were read by the clerk and approved." If the regular clerk is absent, insert after the words "in the chair" the following: "The clerk being absent, Robert Smith was appointed clerk *pro tem.* The minutes were then read and approved." If the minutes were not read, say "The reading of the minutes was dispensed with." The above form will show the essentials, which are as follows: (*a*) The kind of meeting, "regular" [or stated] or "special," or "adjourned regular" or "adjourned special;" (*b*) name of the assembly; (*c*) date and place of

---

* See Clerk and Minutes, in Part II, § 51.

meeting (excepting when the place is always the same); (*d*) the fact of the presence of the regular chairman and clerk, or in their absence the names of their substitutes; (*e*) whether the minutes of the previous meeting were approved.

The minutes should be signed by the person who acted as clerk for that meeting; in some societies the Chairman must also sign them. When published, they should be signed by both officers.

In keeping the minutes much depends upon the kind of meeting, and whether the minutes are to be published. Under no circumstances, however, should the clerk criticize in the minutes, either favorably or otherwise, anything said or done in the meeting. If they are to be published, it is often of far more interest to know what was said by the leading speakers than to know what routine business was done, and what resolutions adopted. In such cases the duties of the secretary are arduous, and he should have at least one assistant.

In ordinary society meetings and meetings of boards of managers and trustees, on the contrary, there is no object in reporting the debates; the duty of the clerk, in such cases, is mainly to record what is " done " by the assembly, not what is said by the members. Unless there is a rule to the contrary, he should enter every Principal Motion [§ 6] that is before the assembly, whether it is adopted or rejected; and where there is a division [see Voting, § 38], or where the vote is by ballot, he should enter the number of votes on each side; and when the voting is by yeas and nays [§ 38], he should enter a list of the names of those voting on each side. He should indorse on the reports of committees the date of their reception, and what further action was taken upon them, and preserve them among the records, for which he is responsible. He should, in the minutes, make a brief summary of a report* that has been agreed to, except where it contains resolutions, in which case the resolutions will be entered in full as adopted by the assembly, and not as if it was the report accepted. The proceedings of the committee of the whole [§ 32], or while acting informally [§ 33], should not be entered on the minutes. Before an adjournment without day it is customary to read over the minutes

---

* If the report is of great importance the assembly should order it " to be entered on the minutes," in which case the clerk copies it in full upon the record.

for approval, if the next meeting of the board or society will not occur for a long period. Where the regular meetings are not separated by too great a time, the minutes are read at the next meeting.

The clerk should, previous to each meeting, for the use of the Chairman, make out an order of business [§ 44], showing in their exact order what is necessarily to come before the assembly. He should also have, at each meeting, a list of all standing committees, and such select committees as are in existence at the time. When a committee is appointed, he should hand the names of the committee, and all papers referred to it, to the chairman, or some other of its members.

Art. VIII.   Miscellaneous.

[§§ 42–45.]

42. A Session of an assembly is a meeting* which, though it may last for days, is virtually *one meeting*, as a session of a convention; or even months, as a session of Congress;

---

* In this Manual the term *Meeting* is used to denote an assembling together of the members of a deliberative assembly for

it terminates by an "adjournment without day."
The intermediate adjournments from day to
day, or the recesses taken during the day, do
not destroy the continuity of the meeting—
they in reality constitute one session. Any
meeting which is not an adjournment of another meeting commences a new session. In
the case of a permanent society, having regular
meetings every week, month or year, for example, each meeting constitutes a separate session of the society, which session, however,

---

any length of time, during which there is no separation of the
members by adjournment. An adjournment to meet again at
some other time, even the same day, terminates the meeting, but
not the session, which latter includes all the adjourned meetings.
The next meeting, in this case, would be an "adjourned meeting" of the same session.

A "*meeting*" of an assembly is terminated by a temporary
adjournment; a "*session*" of an assembly ends with an adjournment without day, and may consist of many meetings. Sometimes a *recess* is taken for a few minutes, and this does not
terminate the "meeting."

In ordinary practice a meeting is closed by moving simply
"to adjourn;" the society meet again at the time provided either
by their rules or by a resolution of the society. If they do not
meet till the time for the next regular meeting, as provided in
the By-Laws, then the adjournment closed the session, and was
in effect an adjournment without day. If, however, they had
previously fixed the time for the next meeting, either by a direct
vote or by adopting a programme of exercises covering several
meetings, or even days, in either case the adjournment is in effect
to a certain day, and does not close the session. When an assembly has meetings for several days consecutively, they all constitute one session.

can be prolonged by adjourning to another day.

If a Principal Motion [§ 6] is indefinitely postponed or rejected at one session, while it cannot be introduced again at the same session [see Renewal of a Motion, § 26], it can be at the next, unless it is prohibited by a rule of the assembly.

No one session of the assembly can interfere with the rights of the assembly at any future session,* unless it is expressly so provided in their Constitution, By-Laws, or Rules of Order, all of which are so guarded (by requiring notice of amendments, and at least a two-thirds vote for their adoption) that they are not subject to sudden changes, but may be considered as expressing the deliberate views of the whole society, rather than the opinions or wishes of any particular meeting. Thus, if the presiding officer were ill, it would not be competent for one session of the assembly to elect a chairman to hold office longer than that session, as it cannot control or dic-

---

* Any one session can adopt a rule or resolution of a permanent nature, and it continues in force until at some future session it is rescinded. But these Standing Rules [§ 49], as they are termed, do not interfere with future sessions, because at any moment a majority can suspend or rescind them, or adopt new ones.

tate to the next session of the assembly. By
going through the prescribed routine of an
election to fill the vacancy, giving whatever
notice is required, it could then legally elect a
chairman to hold office while the vacancy
lasted. So it is improper for an assembly to
postpone anything to a day beyond the next
succeeding session, and thus attempt to prevent the next session from considering the
question. On the other hand, it is not permitted to move a reconsideration [§ 27] of a
vote taken at a previous session [though the
motion to reconsider can be called up, provided it was made at the last meeting of the
previous session]. Committees can be appointed to report at a future session.

NOTE ON SESSION.— In Congress, and in fact all
legislative bodies, the limits of the sessions are
clearly defined; but in ordinary societies having a
permanent existence, with regular meetings more or
less frequent, there appears to be a great deal of confusion upon the subject. Any society is competent
to decide what shall constitute one of its sessions,
but, where there is no rule on the subject, the common parliamentary law would make each of its regular or special meetings a separate session, as they are
regarded in this Manual.

The disadvantages of a rule making a session include all the meetings of an ordinary society, held
during a long time, as one year, are very great. [Ex-
amine Indefinitely Postpone, § 24, and Renewal of a
Motion, § 26.] If members of any society take ad-

vantage of the freedom allowed by considering each regular meeting a separate session, and repeatedly renew obnoxious or unprofitable motions, the society can adopt a rule prohibiting the second introduction of any principal question [§ 6] within, say, three or six months after its rejection, or indefinite postponement, or after the society has refused to consider it. But generally it is better to suppress the motion by refusing to consider it [§ 15].

43. A Quorum of an assembly is such a number as is competent to transact its business. Unless there is a special rule on the subject, the quorum of every assembly is a majority of all the members of the assembly. But whenever a society has a permanent existence it is usual to adopt a much smaller number, the quorum being often less than one-twentieth of its members; this becomes a necessity in most large societies, where only a small fraction of the members are ever present at a meeting.*

---

* While a quorum is competent to transact any business, it is usually not expedient to transact important business unless there is a fair attendance at the meeting, or else previous notice of such action has been given.

In the English Parliament, the House of Lords, consisting of about four hundred and fifty members, can proceed to business if three members are present ; and the House of Commons, with about six hundred and fifty members, requires only forty members for a quorum. The U. S. Constitution [Art. I, Sec. 5] provides that a majority of each House of Congress shall constitute a quorum to do business.

The Chairman should not take the chair till a quorum is present, except where there is no hope of there being a quorum, and then no business can be transacted, except simply to adjourn. So whenever during the meeting there is found not to be a quorum present, the only thing to be done is to adjourn; though, if no question is raised about it, the debate can be continued, but no vote taken, except to adjourn.

In committee of the whole the quorum is the same as in the assembly; in any other committee the majority is a quorum, unless the assembly order otherwise, and it must wait for a quorum before proceeding to business. If the number afterwards should be reduced below a quorum, business is not interrupted, unless a member calls attention to the fact; but no question can be decided except when a quorum is present. Boards of trustees, managers, directors, etc., are on the same footing as committees, in regard to a quorum. Their power is delegated to them as a body, and what number shall be present, in order that they may act as a board, is to be decided by the society that appoints the board. If no quorum is specified, then a majority constitutes a quorum.

44. Order of Business. It is customary for every society having a permanent existence to adopt an order of business for its meetings. When no rule has been adopted, the following is the order:

(1) Reading the Minutes of the previous meeting (and their approval).

(2) Reports of Standing Committees.

(3) Reports of Select Committees.

(4) Unfinished Business.

(5) New Business.

Boards of managers, trustees, etc., come under the head of standing committees. If a subject has been made a "special order" [§ 13] for the day, it takes precedence of all business except reading the minutes. The "orders of the day" [§ 13], which include business postponed to this meeting, come in with unfinished business.

If it is desired to transact business out of its order, it is necessary to suspend the rules [§ 18], which can only be done by a two-thirds vote; but, as each subject comes up, a majority can at once lay it on the table [§ 19], and thus reach any question which they desire to first dispose of.

The order of business, in considering any re-

*port or proposition containing several paragraphs** *or sections,* is as follows:

The whole paper should be read entirely through by the clerk; then the Chairman should read it, or have it read, by paragraphs,† pausing at the end of each, and asking, "Are there any amendments proposed to this paragraph?" If none are offered, he says, "No amendments being offered to this paragraph, the next will be read." He then reads the next, and proceeds thus to the last paragraph, when he states that the whole report or all of the resolutions have been read and are open to amendment. He finally puts the question on agreeing to or adopting the whole paper as amended. If there is a preamble it should be

---

* By "paragraphs" is meant in this rule the separate divisions of the proposition, and they may be Articles, Sections or Paragraphs.

† No vote should be taken on the adoption of the several paragraphs,—one vote being taken finally on the adoption of the whole paper. By not adopting separately the different paragraphs, it is in order, after they have all been amended, to go back and amend any of them still further. In committee a similar paper would be treated the same way [see § 28]. In § 48 (*b*) an illustration is given of the practical application of this section.

If each paragraph or section is adopted separately, it is improper afterwards to vote on the adoption of the whole report, as this would be voting to adopt what has been already adopted in detail. So too it is out of order to go back and amend a paragraph that has been adopted, until after it has been reconsidered.

read after the last paragraph; but if all the resolutions fail, the preamble goes with them, and is not, therefore, read.

If the paper has been reported back by a committee with amendments, the clerk reads only the amendments, and the Chairman then reads the first and puts it to the question, and so on till all the amendments are adopted or rejected, admitting amendments to the committee's amendments, but no others. When through with the committee's amendments, the Chairman pauses for any other amendments to be proposed by the assembly; and when these are voted on he puts the question on agreeing to or adopting the paper as amended. Where the resolutions have been just read by the member presenting them, the reading by the clerk is usually dispensed with without the formality of a vote. By "suspending the rules" [§ 18], or by general consent, a report can be at once adopted without following any of the above routine.

45. Amendments of Rules of Order. These rules can be amended at any regular meeting of the assembly, by a two-thirds vote of the members present, provided the amendment was submitted in writing at the previous

regular meeting.   And no amendment to Constitutions or By-Laws shall be permitted, without at least equal notice and a two-thirds vote.*

---

* Constitutions, By-Laws and Rules of Order should always
prohibit their being amended by less than a two-thirds vote, and
without previous notice of the amendment being given. The
object of this notice is to inform the society that the subject-
matter of the amendment will be up for consideration and action
at a certain time.   It is not to be inferred that notice is required
to amend this amendment; if this were the case it would almost
be impossible to properly amend By-Laws, etc.   But this last
amendment must be germane to the original amendment: no
other amendment is in order or can delay action on the original
amendment. In many cases the By-Laws provide that an amendment must be read at a certain number of regular meetings before
being acted upon : the first reading is by the clerk when it is first
proposed, and after the last reading it is up for action: so that
if it has to be read at three regular meetings, in a society with
regular weekly meetings, action on an amendment would be de-
layed for only two weeks after it was first proposed.

A motion that conflicts with the Constitution, By-Laws,
Rules of Order or Standing Rules, is out of order.   [See note to
§ 49 for the distinctions between these various kinds of rules.]
If the By-Laws should contain rules that it may be desirable to
occasionally suspend, then they should state how they can be
suspended.   If there is no such provision, it is impossible to suspend any rule except such as simply relate to the transaction of
business, if a single member objects [§ 18].   Under such circumstances the English parliamentary law would not permit any rule
to be suspended.

PART II.

ORGANIZATION AND CONDUCT OF BUSINESS.*

Art. IX. Organization and Meetings.

[§§ 46-49.]

46. An Occasional or Mass Meeting.

(*a*) *Organization*. When a meeting is held, which is not one of an organized society, shortly after the time appointed for the meeting, some member of the assembly steps forward and says : " The meeting will please come to order ;

---

* The exact words used by the Chairman or member are in many cases in quotations. It is not to be inferred that these are the only forms permitted, but that these forms are proper and common. They are inserted for the benefit of those unaccustomed to parliamentary forms, and are sufficiently numerous for ordinary meetings.

If pressed for time, the beginner, after reading this section, should begin at § 54, and read the remainder of this second part.

I move that Mr. A act as Chairman of this meeting." Some one else says, " I second the motion." The first member then puts the question to vote, by saying, " It has been moved and seconded that Mr. A act as Chairman of this meeting; those in favor of the motion will say aye ; " and when the affirmative vote is taken, he says, "those opposed will say no." If the majority vote in the affirmative, he says, "The motion is carried ; Mr. A will take the chair." If the motion is lost, he announces that fact, and calls for the nomination of some one else for Chairman, and proceeds with the new nomination as in the first case.*

When Mr. A takes the chair he says, "The first business in order is the election of a secretary." Some one then makes a motion as just described, or he says, "I nominate Mr. B," when the Chairman puts the question as before. Sometimes several names are called out, and

---

* Sometimes a member nominates a Chairman and no vote is taken, the assembly signifying their approval by acclamation. The member who calls the meeting to order, instead of making the motion himself, may act as temporary Chairman, and say : "The meeting will please come to order ; will some one nominate a Chairman ? " He puts the question to vote on the nomination as described above. In large assemblies, the member who nominates, with one other member, frequently conducts the presiding officer to the chair, and the Chairman makes a short speech, thanking the assembly for the honor conferred on him.

the Chairman, as he hears them, says, " Mr. B
is nominated; Mr. C is nominated," etc.; he
then takes a vote on the first one he heard,
putting the question thus: "As many as are in
favor of Mr. B acting as secretary of this meeting will say aye; those opposed will say no."
If the motion is lost the question is put on Mr.
C, and so on, till some one is elected. The
secretary should take his seat near the Chairman, and keep a record of the proceedings, as
described in § 51.

(*b*) *Adoption of Resolutions.* These two officers are all that are usually necessary for a
meeting; so, when the secretary is elected, the
Chairman asks, "What is the further pleasure
of the meeting?" If the meeting is merely a
public assembly called together to consider
some special subject, it is customary at this
stage of the proceedings for some one to offer
a series of resolutions previously prepared, or
else to move the appointment of a committee
to prepare resolutions upon the subject. In
the first case he rises and says, " Mr. Chairman;" the chairman responds, " Mr. C." Mr.
C having thus obtained the floor, then says, " I
move the adoption of the following resolutions," which he then reads and hands to the

chairman;* some one else says, "I second the motion." The chairman sometimes directs the secretary to read the resolutions again, after which he says, "The question is on the adoption of the resolutions just read," and if no one rises immediately, he adds, "Are you ready for the question?" If no one then rises, he says, "As many as are in favor of the adoption of the resolutions just read will say aye;" after the ayes have voted, he says, "As many as are of a contrary opinion will say no;" he then announces the result of the vote as follows: "The motion is carried — the resolutions are adopted," or, "The ayes have it — the resolutions are adopted."

(c) *Committee to draft Resolutions.* If it is preferred to appoint a committee to draft reso-

---

* The practice, in legislative bodies, is to send to the clerk's desk all resolutions, bills, etc., the title of the bill and the name of the member introducing it being indorsed on each. In such bodies, however, there are several clerks and only one chairman. In many assemblies there is but one clerk or secretary, and as he has to keep the minutes there is no reason for his being constantly interrupted to read every resolution offered. In such assemblies, unless there is a rule or established custom to the contrary, it is allowable, and frequently much better, to hand all resolutions, reports, etc., directly to the chairman. If they were read by the member introducing them, and no one calls for another reading, the chairman can omit reading them when he thinks they are fully understood. For the manner of reading and stating the question, when the resolution contains several paragraphs, see § 44.

lutions, a member, after he has addressed the Chair and been recognized, says: "I move that a committee be appointed to draft resolutions expressive of the sense of this meeting on," etc., adding the subject for which the meeting was called. This motion being seconded, the Chairman states the question [§ 65] and asks: "Are you ready for the question?" If no one rises he puts the question, and announces the result; and if it is carried, he asks: "Of how many shall the committee consist?" If only one number is suggested, he announces that the committee will consist of that number; if several numbers are suggested, he states the different ones, and then takes a vote on each, beginning with the largest, until one number is selected.

He then inquires: "How shall the committee be appointed?" This is usually decided without the formality of a vote. The committee may be "appointed" by the Chair; in which case the Chairman names the committee, and no vote is taken; or the committee may be "nominated" by the Chair, or the members of the assembly (no member naming more than one, except by unanimous consent), and then the assembly vote on their appointment. When the Chairman nominates, after stating the names he puts one question on the entire committee, thus: "As many as are in favor of these gentlemen constituting the committee will say aye." If nominations are made by members of the assembly, and more names mentioned than the number of the committee, a separate vote should be taken on each name. (In a mass meeting it is safer to have all committees appointed by the Chairman.)

When the committee are appointed they should at once retire and agree upon a report, which should be written out as described in § 53. During their absence other business may be attended to, or the time may be occupied with hearing addresses. Upon their return* the chairman of the committee (who is the one first named on the committee, and who quite commonly, though not necessarily, is the one who made the motion to appoint the committee,) avails himself of the first opportunity to obtain the floor [see § 2], when he says: " The committee appointed to draft resolutions

---

* If the Chairman sees the committee return to the room, he should, as soon as the member speaking closes, announce that the assembly will now hear the report of the committee on resolutions ; or before this announcement he may ask if the committee is prepared to report.

are prepared to report." The Chairman tells
him that the assembly will now hear the report, which is then read by the chairman of
the committee and handed to the presiding
officer, upon which the committee is dissolved
without any action of the assembly.

A member then moves the "adoption" or
"acceptance" of the report, or that "the resolutions be agreed to," which motions have the
same effect if carried, namely, to make the
resolutions the resolutions of the assembly,
just as if the committee had had nothing to
do with them.* When one of these motions
is made the Chairman acts as stated above,
when the resolutions were offered by a member. If it is not desired immediately to adopt
the resolutions, they can be debated, modified,
their consideration postponed, etc., as explained
in §§ 55–63.

When through with the business for which
the assembly were convened, or when from any
other cause it is desirable to close the meeting,
some one moves "to adjourn;" if the motion
is carried, and no other time for meeting has
been appointed, the chairman says: "The

---

* See note to § 30 for some common errors in acting upon
reports.

motion is carried; this assembly stands adjourned without day." [Another method by which the meeting may be conducted is shown in § 48.]

(*d*) *Additional Officers.* If more officers are required than a chairman and secretary they can be appointed before introducing the resolutions in the manner described for those officers; or the assembly can first form a temporary organization in the manner already described, only adding "pro tem." to the title of the officers, thus: "chairman pro tem." In this latter case, as soon as the secretary pro tem. is elected, a committee is appointed to nominate the permanent officers, as in the case of a convention [§ 47]. Frequently the presiding officer is called the President, and sometimes there is a large number of Vice-Presidents appointed for mere complimentary purposes. The Vice-Presidents in large formal meetings sit on the platform beside the President, and in his absence, or when he vacates the chair, the first on the list that is present should take the chair.

47. Meeting of a Convention or Assembly of Delegates. If the members of the assembly have been elected or appointed

as members, it becomes necessary to know who
are properly members of the assembly and entitled to vote, before the permanent organization is effected. In this case a temporary
organization* is made, as already described, by
the election of a chairman and secretary "pro
tem.," when the chairman announces, "The
next business in order is the appointment of a
committee on credentials." A motion may
then be made covering the entire case, thus:
"I move that a committee of three on the
credentials of members be appointed by the
Chair, and that the committee report as soon
as practicable;" or they may include only one
of these details, thus: "I move that a committee be appointed on the credentials of
members." In either case the Chair proceeds
as already described in the cases of committees
on resolutions [§ 46 (c)].

On the motion to accept the report of the
committee, none can vote except those reported
by the committee as having proper credentials.
The committee, beside reporting a list of members with proper credentials, may report doubtful or contested cases, with recommendations,

---

* Care should be taken to put no one into office, or on a committee, whose right to a seat is doubted.

which the assembly may adopt, or reject, or postpone, etc. Only members whose right to their seats is undisputed, can vote.

The chairman, after the question of credentials is disposed of, at least for the time, announces that "The next business in order is the election of permanent officers of the assembly." Some one then moves the appointment of a committee to nominate the officers, in a form similar to this: "I move that a committee of three be appointed by the Chair to nominate the permanent officers of this convention." This motion is treated as already explained. When the committee make their report, some one moves "that the report of the committee be accepted, and that the officers nominated be declared the officers of this convention." * This motion being carried, the Chairman declares the officers elected, and instantly calls the new presiding officer to the

---

* Where there is any competition for the offices, it is better that they be elected by ballot. In this case, when the nominating committee report, a motion can be made as follows: "I move that the convention now proceed to ballot for its permanent officers;" or, "I move that we now proceed to the election, by ballot, of the permanent officers of this convention." [See § 38 for balloting, and other methods of voting.] The constitutions of permanent societies usually provide that the officers shall be elected by ballot.

chair, and the temporary secretary is at the same time replaced. The convention is now organized for work.

48. A Permanent Society. (*a*) *First Meeting*. When it is desired to form a permanent society, those interested in it should see that only the proper persons are invited to be present at a certain time and place. It is not usual, in mass meetings or meetings called to organize a society, to commence until ten or fifteen minutes after the appointed time, when some one steps forward and says: " The meeting will please come to order; I move that Mr. A act as Chairman of this meeting." Some one "seconds the motion," when the one who made the motion puts it to vote (or, as it is called, "puts the question "), as already described under an "occasional meeting " [§ 46 (*a*)]; and, as in that case, when the Chairman is elected he announces, as the first business in order, the election of a secretary.

After the secretary is elected, the Chairman calls on some member who is most interested in getting up the society to state the object of the meeting. When this member rises he says: " Mr. Chairman." The Chairman then an-

9

nounces his name, when the member proceeds to state the object of the meeting. Having finished his remarks, the Chairman may call on other members to give their opinions upon the subject, and sometimes a particular speaker is called out by members who wish to hear him. The Chairman should observe the wishes of the assembly, and, while being careful not to be too strict, he must not permit any one to occupy too much time and weary the meeting.

When a sufficient time has been spent in this informal way, some one should offer a resolution, so that definite action can be taken. Those interested in getting up the meeting, if it is to be a large one, should have previously agreed upon what is to be done, and be prepared, at the proper time, to offer a suitable resolution, which may be in form similar to this: "Resolved, That it is the sense of this meeting that a society for [state the object of the society] should now be formed in this city." This resolution, when seconded and stated by the Chairman, would be open to debate, and be treated as already described [§ 46 (*b*)]. This preliminary motion could have been offered at the commencement of the meeting, and, if the meeting is a very large one, this would generally be better than to have the informal discussion.

After this preliminary motion has been voted on, or even without waiting for such motion, one like this can be offered: "I move that a committee of five be appointed by the Chair to draft a constitution and by-laws for a society for [here state the object], and that they report at an adjourned meeting of this assembly." This motion can be amended [§ 56] by striking out and adding words, etc., and it is debatable.

When this committee is appointed, the Chairman may inquire: "Is there any other business to be attended to?" or, "What is the further pleasure of the meeting?" When all business is finished, a motion can be made to adjourn, to meet at a certain place and time, which, when seconded and stated by the Chair, is open to debate and amendment. It is usually better to fix the time of the next meeting [see § 63] at an earlier stage of the meeting; and then, when it is desired to close the meeting, move simply "to adjourn," which cannot be amended or debated. When this motion is carried, the Chairman says: "This meeting stands adjourned, to meet at," etc., specifying the time and place of the next meeting.

(*b*) *Second Meeting.** At the next meeting the officers of the previous meeting, if present, serve until the permanent officers are elected. When the hour arrives for the meeting, the chairman standing, says, " The meeting will please come to order ;" as soon as the assembly is seated, he adds, "The secretary will read the minutes of the last meeting." If any one notices an error in the minutes, he can state the fact as soon as the secretary finishes reading them; if there is no objection, without waiting for a motion, the chairman directs the secretary to make the correction. The chairman then says, "If there is no objection the

* Ordinary meetings of a society are conducted like this second meeting, the chairman, however, announcing the business in the order prescribed by the rules of the society [§ 44]. For example, after the minutes are read and approved, he would say, " The next business in order is hearing reports from the standing committees." He may then call upon each committee in their order for a report, thus : " Has the committee on applications for membership any report to make ?" In which case the committee may report, as shown above, or some member of it reply that they have no report to make. Or, when the chairman knows that there are but few if any reports to make, it is better, after making the announcement of the business, for him to ask, " Have these committees any reports to make?" After a short pause, if no one rises to report, he states, " There being no reports from the standing committees, the next business in order is hearing the reports of select committees," when he will act the same as in the case of the standing committees. The chairman should always have a list of the committees, to enable him to call upon them, as well as to guide him in the appointment of new committees.

minutes will stand approved as read" [or corrected," if any corrections have been made].

He announces as the next business in order, "the hearing of the report of the committee on the Constitution and By-Laws." The chairman of the committee, after addressing "Mr. Chairman" and being recognized, reads the committee's report and then hands it to the chairman.* If no motion is made, the chairman says, "You have heard the report read — what order shall be taken upon it?" Or simply inquires, "What shall be done with the report?" Some one moves its adoption, or still better, moves "the adoption of the Constitution reported by the committee," and when seconded, the chairman says, "The question is on the adoption of the Constitution reported by the committee." He then reads the first article of the Constitution, and asks, "Are there any amendments proposed to this article?" If none are offered, after a pause, he reads the next article, and asks the same question, and proceeds thus until he reads the last article, when he says, "The whole Constitution having

---

* In large and formal bodies the chairman, before inquiring what is to be done with the report, usually directs the secretary to read it again. See note to § 30 for a few common errors in acting upon reports of committees. [See also note to § 46 (b).]

been read, it is open to amendment." Now any one can move amendments to any part of the Constitution.

When the Chairman thinks it has been modified to suit the wishes of the assembly, he inquires: "Are you ready for the question?" If no one wishes to speak, he puts the question: "As many as are in favor of adopting the constitution as amended will say aye;" and then, "As many as are opposed will say no." He distinctly announces the result of the vote, which should always be done. If the articles of the constitution are subdivided into sections or paragraphs, then the amendments should be made by sections or paragraphs, instead of by articles.

The Chairman now states that the constitution having been adopted, it will be necessary for those wishing to become members to sign it (and pay the initiation fee, if required by the constitution), and suggests, if the assembly is a large one, that a recess be taken for the purpose. A motion is then made to take a recess for say ten minutes, or until the Constitution is signed. The Constitution being signed, no one is permitted to vote excepting those who have signed it.

The recess having expired, the Chairman calls the meeting to order, and says: "The next business in order is the adoption of By-Laws." Some one moves the adoption of the By-Laws reported by the committee, and they are treated just like the Constitution. The Chairman then asks: "What is the further pleasure of the meeting?" or states that the next business in order is the election of the permanent officers of the society. In either case some one moves the appointment of a committee to nominate the permanent officers of the society, which motion is treated as already described in § 47. As each officer is elected he replaces the temporary one, and when they are all elected the organization is completed.

If the society is one that expects to own real estate, it should be incorporated according to the laws of the State in which it is situated, and for this purpose some one on the committee on the Constitution should consult a lawyer before this second meeting, so that the Constitution may conform to the laws. In this case the trustees are usually instructed to take the proper measures to have the society incorporated.

49. Constitutions, By-Laws, Rules of

Order and Standing Rules. In forming
a Constitution and By-Laws it is always best
to procure copies of those adopted by several
similar societies, and for the committee, after
comparing them, to select one as the basis of
their own, amending each article just as their
own report is amended by the society. When
they have completed amending the Constitution it is adopted by the committee. The By-
Laws are treated in the same way; and then,
having finished the work assigned them, some
one moves "that the committee rise, and that
the chairman (or some other member) report
the Constitution and By-Laws to the assembly." If this is adopted, the Constitution and
By-Laws are written out, and a brief report
made of this form: "Your committee, appointed to draft a Constitution and By-Laws,
would respectfully submit the following, with
the recommendation that they be adopted as
the Constitution and By-Laws of this society,"
which is signed by all the members of the
committee that concur in it. Sometimes the
report is only signed by the chairman of the
committee.

In the organization just given it is assumed
that both a Constitution and By-Laws are

adopted. This is not always done; some societies adopt only a Constitution, and others
only By-Laws. Where both are adopted, the
Constitution usually contains only the following:

(1) Name and object of the society.

(2) Qualification of members.

(3) Officers, their election and duties.

(4) Meetings of the society (only including what
is essential, leaving details to the By-Laws).

(5) How to amend the Constitution.

These can be arranged in five articles, each
article being subdivided into sections. The
Constitution containing nothing but what is
fundamental, it should be made very difficult
to amend; usually, previous notice of the
amendment is required, and also a two-thirds
or three-fourths vote for its adoption [§ 45].
It is better not to require a larger vote than
two-thirds; and, where the meetings are frequent, an amendment should not be allowed
to be made except at a quarterly or annual
meeting, after having been proposed at the
previous quarterly meeting.

The *By-Laws* contain all the other standing
rules of the society, of such importance that
they should be placed out of the power of any
one meeting to modify; or they may omit the

rules relating to the conduct of business in the meetings, which would then constitute the *Rules of Order* of the society.   Every society, in its By-Laws or Rules of Order, should adopt a rule like this: "The rules contained in [specifying the work on parliamentary practice] shall govern the society in all cases to which they are applicable, and in which they are not inconsistent with the Rules of Order (or By-Laws) of this society."   Without such a rule, any one so disposed could cause great trouble in a meeting.

In addition to the Constitution, By-Laws, and Rules of Order, in nearly every society resolutions of a permanent nature are occasionally adopted, which are binding on the society until they are rescinded or modified. These are called *Standing Rules*, and can be adopted by a majority vote at any meeting. After they have been adopted, they cannot be modified at the same session except by a reconsideration [§ 60].   At any future session they can be suspended, modified, or rescinded by a majority vote. The Standing Rules, then, comprise those rules of a society which have been adopted like ordinary resolutions, without the previous notice, etc., required for By-Laws,

and, consequently, future sessions of the society
are at liberty to terminate them whenever they
please. No Standing Rule (or other resolution)
can be adopted which conflicts with the Constitution, By-Laws or Rules of Order.*

Art. X.   Officers and Com-
mittees.

50. Chairman or President. It is the
duty of the Chairman to call the meeting to
order at the appointed time, to preside at all
the meetings, to announce the business before

---

* In practice these various classes of rules are frequently very
much mixed. The Standing Rules of some societies are really
By-Laws, as the society cannot suspend them, nor can they be
amended until previous notice is given. This produces confusion
without any corresponding benefit.

Standing Rules should contain only such rules as are subject
to the will of the majority of any meeting, and which it may be
expedient to change at any time, without the delay incident to
giving previous notice. *Rules of Order* should contain only the
rules relating to the orderly transaction of the business in the
meetings of the society. The *By-Laws* should contain all the
other rules of the society which are of too great importance to
be changed without giving notice to the society of such change ;
provided that the most important of these can be placed in a *Constitution* instead of in the By-Laws. These latter three should
provide for their amendment. The Rules of Order should provide
for their suspension. The By-Laws sometimes provide for the
suspension of certain articles [see note to § 45].

the assembly in its proper order, to state and put all questions properly brought before the assembly, to preserve order and decorum, and to decide all questions of order (subject to an appeal). When he "puts a question" to vote, and when speaking upon an appeal, he should stand;* in all other cases he can sit. In all cases where his vote would affect the result, or where the vote is by ballot, he can vote. When a member rises to speak, he should say, "Mr. Chairman," and the Chairman should reply, "Mr. A;" he should not interrupt a speaker as long as he is in order, but should listen to his speech, which should be addressed to him and not to the assembly. The Chairman should be careful to abstain from the appearance of partisanship, but he has the right to call another member to the chair while he addresses the assembly on a question; when speaking to a question of order he does not leave the chair.

51. The Clerk, Secretary or Recording Secretary, as he is variously called, should keep a record of the proceedings, the character

---

* In meetings of boards of managers, committees, and other small bodies, the chairman usually retains his seat, and even members in speaking do not rise.

of which depends upon the kind of meeting.
In an occasional or mass meeting, the record
usually amounts to nothing, but he should
always record every resolution or motion that
is adopted.

In a convention it is often desirable to keep
a full record for publication, and where it lasts
for several days, it is usual, and generally best,
to appoint one or more assistant clerks. Frequently it is a tax on the judgment of the clerk
to decide what to enter on the record, or the
"Minutes," as it is usually called. Sometimes
the points of each speech should be entered,
and at other times only the remark that the
question was discussed by Messrs. A, B and
C in the affirmative, and Messrs. D, E and
F in the negative. Every resolution that is
adopted should be entered, which can be done
in this form: "On motion of Mr. D it was
resolved that, etc."

Sometimes a convention does its work by
having certain topics previously assigned to
certain speakers, who deliver formal addresses
or essays, the subjects of which are afterwards
open for discussion in short speeches — of five
minutes, for instance. In such cases the minutes are very brief, unless they are to be pub-

lished, when they should contain either the entire addresses, or carefully prepared abstracts of them, and should show the drift of the discussion that followed each one. In permanent societies, where the minutes are not published, they consist of a record of what was done and not what was said, and should be kept in a book. The secretary should never make in the minutes any criticism, either favorable or otherwise, upon anything said or done in a meeting.

The *Form* of the *Minutes* can be as follows:

At a regular meeting of the M. L. Society, held in their hall, on Tuesday evening, March 16, :875, Mr. A in the chair, and Mr. B acting as secretary, the minutes of the previous meeting were read and approved. The committee on Applications reported the names of Messrs. C and D as applicants for membership, and on motion of Mr. F they were admitted as members. The committee on ——— reported through Mr. G a series of resolutions, which were thoroughly discussed and amended, and finally adopted, as follows:

Resolved, That   *   *   *   *   *   *
*   *   *   *   *   *   *   *   *   *
On motion of Mr. L the society adjourned.

L—— B——,
Secretary.

If the proceedings are to be published, the secretary should always examine the published proceedings of similar meetings, so as to conform to the custom, excepting where it is manifestly improper.

The Constitution, By-Laws, Rules of Order and Standing Rules should all be written in one book, leaving every other page blank; and whenever an amendment is made to any of them, it should be immediately entered on the page opposite to the article amended, with a reference to the date and page of the minutes where is recorded the action of the society.

The secretary has the custody of all papers belonging to the society, not specially under charge of any other officer. Sometimes his duties are also of a financial kind, when he should make such reports as are prescribed in the next section.

52. Treasurer. The duties of this officer vary in different societies. In probably the majority of cases he acts as a banker, merely holding the funds deposited with him, and paying them out on the order of the society signed by the secretary. His annual report, which is always required, in this case consists of merely a statement of the amount on hand at the commencement of the year, the amount received during the year (stating from what sources received), the total amount paid out by order of the society, and the balance on hand. When this report is presented it is referred to an "auditing committee," consisting of one or two persons, who examine the treasurer's books and vouchers, and certify on his report that they "have examined his accounts and vouchers and find them correct, and the balance on hand is," etc., stating the amount on hand. The auditing committee's report being accepted is equivalent to a resolution of the society to the same effect, namely, that the treasurer's report is correct.

In the case here supposed the real financial statement is made either by the board of trustees, or by the secretary or some other officer, according to the Constitution of the society. The principles involved are, that every officer who receives money is to account for it in a report to the society, and that whatever officer is responsible for the disbursements shall report them to the society. If the secretary, as in many societies, is really responsible for the expenses, the treasurer merely paying upon his order, then the secretary should make a full report of these expenses, so classified as to enable the society to readily see the amounts expended for various purposes.

It should always be remembered that the financial report is made for the information of members. The details of dates and separate payments for the same object are a hinderance to its being understood, and are useless, as it is the duty of the auditing committee to examine into the details and see if the report is correct.

Every disbursing officer should be careful to get a receipt whenever he makes a payment; these receipts should be preserved in regular order, as they are the vouchers for the payments, which must be examined by the auditing committee. Disbursing officers cannot be too careful in keeping their accounts, and they should insist upon having their accounts audited every time they make a report, as by this means any error is quickly detected and may be corrected. When the society has accepted the auditing committee's report that the financial report is correct, the disbursing officer is relieved from the responsibility of the past, and if his vouchers were lost afterwards it would cause no trouble. The best form for these financial reports depends upon the kind of society, and is best determined by examining those made in similar societies.

10

The following form can be varied to suit most cases [when the statement of receipts and expenses is very long, it is often desirable to specify the amounts received from one or two particular sources, which can be done immediately after stating the total receipts; the same course can be taken in regard to the expenditures]:

Treasurer's Report.

The undersigned, Treasurer of the M. L. Society, begs leave to submit the following annual report:

The balance on hand at the commencement of the year was ——— dollars and ——— cents. There was received from all sources during the year ——— dollars and ——— cents; during the same time the expenses amounted to ——— dollars and —— cents, leaving a balance on hand of ——— dollars and —— cents.

The annexed statement of receipts and expenditures will show in detail the sources from which the receipts were obtained, and the objects to which the expenditures have been applied.

All of which is respectfully submitted.

S—— M——,

Treasurer M. L. S.

The "Statement of receipts and expenditures" can be made by simply giving a list of receipts, followed by a list of expenses, and finishing up with the balance on hand. The auditing committee's certificate to the correctness of the account should be written on the statement. Often the statement is made out in the form of an account, as follows:

Dr. The M. L. S. in acct. with S. M., Treas'r. *Cr.*

1875.			1875.		
Dec. 31.	To rent of hall	$500 00	Jan. 1.	By balance on hand from last year's account	$ 21 13
	" gas	80 00	Dec 31.	By initiation fees	95 00
	" stationery	26 50		" members' dues	860 00
	" janitor	360 00		" fines	15 00
	" balance on hand	24 63			
		$991 13			$991 13

We do hereby certify that we have examined the accounts and vouchers of the treasurer, and find them correct; and that the balance in his hands is twenty-four dollars and sixty-three cents.

$$\left. \begin{array}{c} \text{R. V.,} \\ \text{J. L.,} \end{array} \right\} \textit{Audit. Com.}$$

53. Committees. In small assemblies, especially in those where but little business is done, there is not much need of committees. But in large assemblies, or in those doing a great deal of business, committees are of the utmost importance. When a committee is properly selected, in nine cases out of ten its action decides that of the assembly. A committee for *action* should be small, and consist only of those heartily in favor of the proposed action. A committee for deliberation or investigation, on the contrary, should be larger, and represent all parties in the assembly, so that its opinion will carry with it as great weight as possible. The usefulness of the committee will be greatly impaired if any important faction of the assembly be unrepresented on the committee. The appointment of a committee is fully explained in § 46 (*c*).

The first member named on a committee is their chairman, and it is his duty to call together the committee and preside at their meetings. If he is absent, or from any cause fails or declines to call a meeting, it is the duty of the committee to assemble on the call of any two of their members. The committee are a miniature assembly, only being able to act when a quorum is present. If a paper is referred to them, they must not deface it in any way, but write their amendments on a separate sheet. If they originate the paper, all amendments must be incorporated in it. When they originate the paper, usually one member has previously prepared a draft, which is read entirely through, and then read by paragraphs, the chairman pausing after each paragraph, and asking: "Are there any amendments proposed to this paragraph?" No vote is taken on the adoption of the separate paragraphs; but, after the whole paper has been read in this way, it is open to amendment, generally by striking out any paragraph or inserting new ones, or by substituting an entirely new paper for it. When it has been amended to suit the committee, they should adopt it as their report, and direct the chairman or some other member to report it to the assembly. It is then written out, usually commencing in a style similar to this: " The committee to which was referred [state the matter referred], beg leave to submit the following report; " or, "Your committee appointed to [specify the object], would respectfully report," etc. It usually closes thus: "All of which is respectfully submitted," followed by the signatures of all the members concurring in the report, or sometimes by only that of the chairman.

If the minority submit a report, it commences thus: " The undersigned, a minority of the committee appointed," etc., continuing as the regular report of the committee. After the committee's report has been read it is usual to allow the minority to present their report; but it cannot be acted upon except by a motion to substitute it for the report of the committee. When the committee's report is

read they are discharged without any motion.
A motion to refer the paper back to the same
committee (or to recommit), if adopted, re-
vives the committee.

Art. XI. Introduction of Busi-
ness.

54. Any member wishing to bring business
before the assembly should, unless it is very
simple, write down, in the form of a motion,
what he would like to have the assembly adopt,
thus:

Resolved, That the thanks of this convention be
tendered to the citizens of this community for their
hearty welcome and generous hospitality.

When there is no other business before the
assembly, he rises and addresses the chairman
by his title, thus: "Mr. Chairman," who immediately recognizes him by announcing his
name.*   He then, having the floor, says, "I
move the adoption of the following resolution,"

---

* If the chairman has any special title (as President, for instance), he should be addressed by it, thus: "Mr. President."
Sometimes the chairman recognizes the speaker by merely bowing
to him, but the proper course is to announce his name.

which he reads and hands to the chairman.*
Some one else seconds the motion, and the
chairman says, "It has been moved and seconded that the following resolution be adopted,"
when he reads the resolution; or he may read
the resolution and then state the question thus;
"The question is on the adoption of the resolution just read." The merits of the resolution
are then open to discussion, but before any
member can discuss the question or make any
motion, he must first obtain the floor as just
described. After the chairman states the question, if no one rises to speak, or when he thinks
the debate closed, he asks, "Are you ready for
the question?"† If no one then rises, he puts
the question in a form similar to the following:
"The question is on the adoption of the resolution which you have heard read; as many as
are in favor of its adoption will say aye." When
the ayes have voted, he says, "As many as are
of a contrary opinion will say no." He then
announces the result, stating that the motion

---

* Or, when he is recognized by the chair, he may say that he
wishes to offer the following resolutions, which he reads and then
moves their adoption. In very large bodies the name of the mover
should be indorsed on the written resolutions, especially if much
business is to be transacted.

† See second note to § 65.

is carried, or lost, as the case may be, in the following form: "The motion is carried — the resolution is adopted;" or, "The ayes have it, — the resolution is adopted." A majority of the votes cast is sufficient for the adoption of any motion, excepting those mentioned in § 39. [For other forms of stating and putting questions see § 65. For other illustrations of the common practice in introducing business, and in making various motions, see §§ 46–48.]

Art. XII.   Motions.

55. Motions Classified According to their Object. Instead of immediately adopting or rejecting a resolution as originally submitted, it may be desirable to dispose of it in some other way, and for this purpose various motions have come into use, which can be made while a resolution is being considered, and, for the time being, supersede it.   No one can make any of these motions while another member has the floor, excepting as shown in the Table of Rules: the circumstances under which each motion can be made are shown in the Order of Precedence of Motions, p. 10.

The following list comprises most of these motions, arranged in eight classes, according to the object for which each motion is used:

MOTIONS CLASSIFIED ACCORDING TO THEIR OBJECT.

[The object to be attained is printed thus: "(2) To defer action;" the motions to accomplish this object are printed in *Italics* under the object, and marked (*a*), (*b*), etc.; the difference in the use of these motions is shown in the section referred to.]

(1) To Modify or Amend ....[§ 56]
    (*a*) *Amend.*
    (*b*) *Commit.*

(2) To Defer Action........................[§ 57]
    (*a*) *Postpone to a Certain Time.*
    (*b*) *Lie on the Table.*

(3) To Suppress Debate ....[§ 58]
    (*a*) *Previous Question.*
    (*b*) *An Order Limiting or Closing Debate.*

(4) To Suppress the Question ....[§ 59]
    (*a*) *Objection to its Consideration.*
    (*b*) *Postpone Indefinitely.*
    (*c*) *Lie on the Table.*

(5) To Consider a Question the Second Time..[§ 60]
    (*a*) *Reconsider.*

(6) Order and Rules........................[§ 61]
    (*a*) *Orders of the Day.*
    (*b*) *Special Orders.*
    (*c*) *Suspension of the Rules.*
    (*d*) *Questions of Order.*
    (*e*) *Appeal.*

56. To Modify or Amend. (a) *Amend.* If it is desired to modify the question in any way, the proper motion to make is "to amend," either by "adding" words, or by "striking out" words; or by "striking out certain words and inserting others;" or by "substituting" a different motion on the same subject for the one before the assembly; or by "dividing the question" into two or more questions, as the mover specifies, so as to get a separate vote on any particular point or points. Sometimes the enemies of a measure seek to amend it in such a way as to divide its friends, and thus defeat it.

When the amendment has been moved and seconded, the Chairman should always state the question distinctly, so that every one may know exactly what is before them, reading first the paragraph which it is proposed to amend; then the words to be struck out, if there are any; next, the words to be inserted, if any; and finally, the paragraph as it will stand if the amendment is adopted. He then states that the question is on the adoption of the amendment, which is open to debate, the remarks being confined to the merits of the amendment, only going into the main question so far as is necessary in order to ascertain the propriety of adopting the amendment.

This amendment can be amended, but an "amendment of an amendment" cannot be amended. None of the undebatable motions mentioned in § 35, except to fix the time to which to adjourn, to extend the limits of debate, and to close or limit debate, can be amended, nor can the motion to postpone indefinitely.

(b) *Commit.* If the original question is not well digested, or needs more amendment than can well be made in the assembly, it is usual to move "to refer it to a committee." This motion can be made while an amendment is pending, and it opens the whole merits of the question to debate. This motion can be amended by specifying the number of the committee, or how they shall be appointed, or when they shall report, or by giving them any other instructions. [See § 53 on committees, and § 46 (c) on their appointment.]

57 To Defer Action. (*a*) *Postpone to a Certain Time.* If it is desired to defer action upon a question till a particular time, the proper motion to make is "to postpone it to that time." This motion allows of but limited debate, which must be confined to the propriety of the postponement to that time; it can be amended by altering the time, and this amendment allows of the same debate. The time specified must not be beyond that session [§ 42] of the assembly, except it be the next session, in which case it comes up with the unfinished business at the next session. This motion can be made when a motion to amend, or to commit, or to postpone indefinitely, is pending.

(*b*) *Lie on the Table.* Instead of postponing a question to a particular time, it may be desired to lay it aside temporarily until some other question is disposed of, retaining the privilege of resuming its consideration at any time.* The only way to accomplish this is to

---

* In Congress this motion is commonly used to defeat a measure, though it does not prevent a majority from taking it up at any other time. Some societies prohibit a question from being taken from the table, except by a two-thirds vote. This rule deprives the society of the advantages of the motion "to lie on the table," because it would not be safe to lay a question aside temporarily, if one-third of the assembly were opposed to the measure, as that one-third could prevent its ever being taken from

move that the question "lie on the table."
This motion allowing of neither debate nor
amendment, the Chairman immediately puts
the question; if carried, the whole matter is
laid aside till the assembly vote to "take it
from the table" (which latter motion is undebatable and possesses no privilege). Sometimes this motion is used to suppress a measure, as shown in § 59 (c).

58. To Suppress Debate.* (a) *Previous
Question.* While, as a general rule, free debate
is allowed upon every motion,† which, if adopted, has the effect of adopting the original question or removing it from before the assembly for
the session, yet, to prevent a minority from
making an improper use of this privilege, it is
necessary to have methods by which debate
can be closed and final action can at once be
taken upon a question.

---

the table. A bare majority should not have the power, in ordinary societies, to adopt or reject a question, or prevent its
consideration, without debate. [See note at end of § 35, on the
principles involved in making questions undebatable.]

* These motions are strictly for closing or limiting debate, and
may be used by either the friends or enemies of a measure. The
enemies of a measure may also close debate by suppressing the
question itself, as shown in § 59 (a, c).

† Except an "objection to the consideration of the question"
[§ 59 (a)]. See note to § 35 for a full discussion of this subject
of debate.

To accomplish this, when any debatable question is before the assembly, it is only necessary for some one to obtain the floor and "call for the previous question;" this call being seconded, the Chairman, as it allows of no debate, instantly puts the question thus: "Shall the main question be now put?" If this is carried by a two-thirds vote [§ 39] all debate instantly ceases, excepting that in case the pending measure has been reported from a committee the member reporting it is, as in all other cases, entitled to the floor to close the debate; after which the Chairman immediately puts the questions to the assembly, first on the motion to commit, if it is pending; if this is carried, of course the subject goes to the committee; if, however, it fails, the vote is next taken on amendments, and finally on the resolution as amended.

If a motion to postpone, either definitely or indefinitely, or a motion to reconsider, or an appeal is pending, the previous question is exhausted by the vote on the postponement, reconsideration or appeal, and does not cut off debate upon any other motions that may be pending. If the call for the previous question fails — that is, the debate is not cut off —

the debate continues the same as if this motion
had not been made. The previous question
can be called for simply on an amendment;
and after the amendment has been acted upon,
the main question is again open to debate.*

(*b*) *An Order Limiting or Closing Debate.*
Sometimes, instead of cutting off debate entirely, by ordering the previous question, it is
desirable to allow of but very limited debate.
In this case a motion is made to limit the
time allowed each speaker, or the number of
speeches on each side, or to appoint a time
at which debate shall close and the question
be put. The motion may be made to limit
debate on an amendment, in which case the
main question would afterwards be open to
debate and amendment; or it may be made
simply on an amendment of an amendment.

In ordinary societies, where harmony is so
important, a two-thirds vote should be required for the adoption of any of the above
motions to cut off or limit debate.†

---

* As the Previous Question is so generally misunderstood, it
would be well to read also what is said upon this subject in § 20.

† In the House of Representatives these motions require only
a majority vote for their adoption. In the Senate, on the contrary, not even two-thirds of the members can force a measure
to its passage without allowing debate, the Senate rules not
recognizing the above motions.

59. To Suppress the Question. (*a*) *Objection to the Consideration of a Question.* Sometimes a resolution is introduced that the assembly do not wish to consider at all, because it is profitless, or irrelevant to the objects of the assembly, or for other reasons. The proper course to pursue in such case is for some one, as soon as it is introduced, to "object to the consideration of the question." This objection not requiring a second, the Chairman immediately puts the question: "Will the assembly consider this question?" If decided in the negative by a two-thirds vote, the question is immediately dismissed, and cannot be again introduced during that session. This objection must be made when the question is first introduced, before it has been debated, and it can be made when another member has the floor.

(*b*) *Postpone Indefinitely.* After the question has been debated, the proper motion to use in order to suppress the question for the session, is to postpone indefinitely. It cannot be made while any motion except the original or main question is pending, but it can be made after an amendment has been acted upon, and the main question, as amended, is before the assembly. It opens the merits of the main question to debate to as great an extent as if the main question were before the assembly. On account of these two facts, in assemblies with short sessions it is not very useful, as the same result can usually be more easily attained by the next motion.

(c) *Lie on the Table.* If there is no possibility during the remainder of the session of obtaining a majority vote for taking up the question, then the quickest way of suppressing it is to move "that the question lie on the table;" which, allowing of no debate, enables the majority to instantly lay the question on the table, from which it cannot be taken without their consent.

From its high rank [see p. 10] and undebatable character, this motion is very commonly used to suppress a question, but, as shown in § 57 (b). its effect is merely to lay the question aside till the assembly choose to consider it, and it only suppresses the question so long as there is a majority opposed to its consideration.

60. To Consider a Question a Second Time. *Reconsider.* When a question has been once adopted, rejected or suppressed it cannot be again considered during that session [§ 42],

except by a motion to "reconsider the vote" on
that question.   This motion can only be made
by one who voted on the prevailing side, and
on the day the vote was taken which it is proposed to reconsider.*   It can be made and
entered on the minutes in the midst of debate,
even when another member has the floor, but
cannot be considered until there is no question
before the assembly, when, if called up, it takes
precedence of every motion except to adjourn
and to fix the time to which the assembly shall
adjourn.

A motion to reconsider a vote on a debatable question, opens to debate the entire merits
of the original motion.   If the question to be
reconsidered is undebatable, then the reconsideration is undebatable.

If the motion to reconsider is carried, the
Chairman announces that the question now
recurs on the adoption of the question the
vote on which has been just reconsidered; the
original question is now in exactly the same
condition that it was in before the first vote

---

* In Congress it can be made on the same or succeeding day ;
and if the yeas and nays were not taken on the vote, any one can
move the reconsideration.   The yeas and nays are, however, ordered on all important votes in Congress, which is not the case in
ordinary societies.

was taken on its adoption, and must be disposed of by a vote.

When a motion to reconsider is entered on the minutes, it need not be called up by the mover till the next meeting, on a succeeding day.* If he fails to call it up then, any one else can do so. But should there be no succeeding meeting, either adjourned or regular, within a month, then the effect of the motion to reconsider terminates with the adjournment of the meeting at which it was made, and any one can call it up at that meeting.

In general no motion (except to adjourn) that has been once acted upon can again be considered during the same session, except by a motion to reconsider. [The motion to adjourn can be renewed if there has been progress in business or debate, and it cannot be reconsidered.] But this rule does not prevent the renewal of any of the motions mentioned in § 7, provided the question before the assembly has in any way changed; for in this

---

* If the assembly has not adopted these or similar rules, this paragraph would not apply ; but this motion to reconsider would, like any other motion, fall to the ground if not acted upon before the close of the session at which the original vote was adopted.

case, while the motions are nominally the same, they are in fact different.*

61. Order and Rules. (*a*) *Orders of the Day.* Sometimes an assembly decides that certain questions shall be considered at a particular time, and when that time arrives those questions constitute what is termed the "orders of the day;" and if any member "calls for the orders of the day," as it requires no second, the Chairman immediately puts the question thus: "Will the assembly now proceed to the orders of the day?" If carried, the subject under consideration is laid aside, and the questions appointed for that time are taken up in their order. When the time arrives the Chairman may state that fact, and put the above question without waiting for a motion; or, he can announce the orders of the day without taking any vote, if no one objects. If the motion fails, the call for the orders of the day

---

* Thus to move to postpone a resolution is a different question from moving to postpone it after it has been amended. A motion to suspend the rules for a certain purpose cannot be renewed at the same meeting, but can be at an adjourned meeting. A call for the orders of the day, that has been negatived, cannot be renewed while the question then before the assembly is still under consideration. [See § 27 for many peculiarities of this motion.]

cannot be renewed till the subject then before the assembly is disposed of.*

(*b*) *Special Order*. If a subject is of such importance that it is desired to consider it at a special time, in preference to the orders of the day and established order of business, then a motion should be made to make the question a "special order" for that particular time. This motion requires a two-thirds vote for its adoption, because it is really a suspension of the rules, and it is in order whenever a motion to suspend the rules is in order. If a subject is a special order for a particular day, then on that day it supersedes all business except the reading of the minutes. A special order can be postponed by a majority vote. If two special orders are made for the same day, the one first made takes precedence.

(*c*) *Suspension of the Rules*. It is necessary for every assembly, if discussion is allowed, to have rules to prevent its time being wasted, and to enable it to accomplish the object for which the assembly was organized; and yet at times their best interests are subserved by suspending their rules temporarily. In order to do this some one makes a motion "to suspend

---

* See § 13 for a fuller explanation.

the rules that interfere with," etc., stating the object of the suspension. If this motion is carried by a two-thirds vote, then the particular thing for which the rules were suspended can be done. By "general consent," that is, if no one objects, the rules relating to the transaction of business can at any time be ignored without the formality of a motion.

(*d*) *Questions of Order.* It is the duty of the Chairman to enforce the rules and preserve order, and when any member notices a breach of order he can call for the enforcement of the rules. In such cases, when he rises he usually says: "Mr. Chairman, I rise to a point of order." The Chairman then directs the speaker to take his seat, and, having heard the point of order, decides the question and permits the first speaker to resume his speech, directing him to abstain from any conduct that was decided to be out of order. When a speaker has transgressed the rules of decorum he cannot continue his speech if any one objects, unless permission is granted him by a vote of the assembly. Instead of the above method, when a member uses improper language, some one says: "I call the gentleman to order," when the Chairman decides as before whether the language is disorderly.

(e) *Appeal.* While on all questions of order, and of interpretation of the rules, and of priority of business, it is the duty of the Chairman to first decide the question, it is the privilege of any member to "appeal from the decision." If the appeal is seconded, the Chairman states his decision, and that it has been appealed from, and then states the question thus : "Shall the decision of the Chair stand as the judgment of the assembly [or society, convention, etc.] ? "

The Chairman can then, without leaving the chair, state the reasons for his decision, after which it is open to debate (no member speaking more than once), excepting in the following cases, when it is undebatable : (1) When it relates to transgressions of the rules of speaking, or to some indecorum, or to the priority of business ; and (2) when the previous question was pending at the time the question of order was raised. After the vote is taken, the Chairman states that the decision of the Chair is sustained, or reversed, as the case may be.

62. Miscellaneous. (a) *Reading of Papers* and (b) *Withdrawal of a Motion.* If a speaker wishes to read a paper, or a member to withdraw his motion after it has been stated by the Chair, it is necessary, if any one objects, to make a motion to grant the permission.

(*c*) *Questions of Privilege.* Should any disturbance occur during the meeting, or anything affecting the rights of the assembly, or any of the members, any member may "rise to a question of privilege," and state the matter, which the Chairman decides to be, or not to be, a matter of privilege.* (From the Chairman's decision of course an appeal can be taken.) If the question is one of privilege, it supersedes, for the time being, the business before the assembly; its consideration can be postponed to another time, or the previous question can be ordered on it so as to stop debate, or it can be laid on the table, or referred to a committee to examine and report upon it. As soon as the question of privilege is in some way disposed of, the debate which was interrupted is resumed.

63. To Close the Meeting. (*a*) *Fix the Time to which to Adjourn.*

If it is desired to have an adjourned meeting of the assembly, it is best some time before its close to move, "That when this assembly adjourns, it adjourns to meet at such a time,"

---

*A personal explanation is not a matter of privilege. It can be made only by leave of the assembly implied or expressed.

specifying the time. This motion can be amended by altering the time, but if made when another question is before the assembly, neither the motion nor the amendment can be debated. If made when no other business is before the assembly, it stands as any other main question, and can be debated. This motion can be made even while the assembly is voting on the motion to adjourn, but not when another member has the floor.

(*b*) *Adjourn.* In order to prevent an assembly from being kept in session an unreasonably long time, it is necessary to have a rule limiting the time that the floor can be occupied by any one member at one time.* When it is desired to close the meeting, unless the member who has the floor will yield it, the only resource is to wait till his time expires, and then a member who gets the floor should move "to adjourn." The motion being seconded, the Chairman instantly puts the question, as it allows of no amendment or debate ; and if decided in the affirmative he says, "The motion is carried; this assembly stands adjourned." If the assembly is one that will have no other meeting, instead of "adjourned," he says, "ad-

---

* Ten minutes is allowed by these rules.

journed without day," or "*sine die*." If previously it had been decided when they adjourned to adjourn to a particular time, then he
states that the assembly stands adjourned to
that time.   If the motion to adjourn is qualified by specifying the time, as, "to adjourn to
to-morrow evening," it cannot be made when
any other question is before the assembly ; like
any other main motion, it can then be amended
and debated.*

Art. XIII.   Miscellaneous.

64. Debate. All remarks must be addressed to the chairman and confined to the
question before the assembly, avoiding all
personalities and reflections upon any one's
motives.   It is usual for permanent assemblies to adopt rules limiting the number of
times any one can speak to the same question, and the time allowed for each speech,†
as otherwise one member, while he could
speak only once to the same question, might

---

* See § 11 for effect of an adjournment upon unfinished business.

† In Congress, the House of Representatives allows from each
member only one speech of one hour's length : the Senate allows
two speeches without limit as to length.

defeat a measure by prolonging his speech, and declining to yield the floor except for a motion to adjourn. In ordinary assemblies two speeches should be allowed each member (except upon an appeal), and these rules also limit the time for each speech to ten minutes. A majority can permit a member to speak oftener or longer whenever it is desired, and the motion granting such permission cannot be debated. However, if greater freedom is wanted, it is only necessary to consider the question informally, or if the assembly is large, to go into committee of the whole.* If, on the other hand, it is desired to limit the debate more, or close it altogether, it can be done by a two-thirds vote, as shown in § 58 (*b*).

65. Forms of Stating and Putting Questions. Whenever a motion has been made and seconded, it is the duty of the Chairman, if the motion is in order, to state the question, so that the assembly may know what question is before them. The seconding of a motion is required to prevent the introduction of a question when only one member is in favor of it, and consequently but little attention is

---

* See §§ 32, 33.

paid to mere routine motions, or when it is evident that many are in favor of the motion; in such cases the Chairman assumes that the motion is seconded.

Often in routine work the Chairman puts the question without waiting for even a motion,* as few persons like to make such formal motions, and much time would be wasted by waiting for them (but the Chairman can only do this as long as no one objects). The following motions, however, do not have to be seconded: (a) a call for the orders of the day; (b) a call to order, or the raising of any question of order; and (c) an objection to the consideration of a question.

One of the commonest forms of stating a question is to say that, "It is moved and seconded that," and then give the motion; or, in case of resolutions, it might be stated in this way (after they have been read): "The ques-

---

* A presiding officer can frequently expedite business by not waiting for a motion or even taking a vote on a question of routine. In such a case he announces that if there is no objection such will be considered the action of the assembly. For example, when the treasurer's report is read he can say, "If there is no objection the report will be referred to an auditing committee, consisting of Messrs. A and B," — adding, after a moment's pause, "It is so referred."

tion is on the adoption of the resolutions just read."

In some cases, in order to state the question clearly, the Chairman should do much more than merely repeat the motion, and say that the question is on its adoption. In the case of an appeal, he should state the decision of the Chair (and, if he thinks proper, the reasons for it), and that the decision has been appealed from; he then says, "The question is, shall the decision of the Chair stand as the judgment of the assembly?" In stating the question on an amendment, the Chairman should read (1) the passage to be amended; (2) the words to be struck out, if any; (3) the words to be inserted, if any; and (4) the whole passage as it will stand if the amendment is adopted; he then states the question in a form similar to this: "The question is, shall the word *censure* be inserted in the resolution in the place of the word *thanks?*" As soon as a vote is taken, he should immediately state the question then before the assembly, if there be any. Thus, if an amendment has been voted on, the Chairman announces the result, and then says: "The question now recurs on the resolution," or, "on the resolution as amended," as the case may be. So, if an amendment is reconsidered, the Chairman should announce the result of the vote and state the question before the assembly in a form similar to this: "The motion is carried — the vote on the amendment is reconsidered; the question recurs on the adoption of the amendment."

After stating the question on a motion that can be debated or amended, the Chairman, unless some one immediately rises, asks: "Are you ready for the question?"* When the Chairman thinks the debate is closed, he again inquires: "Are you ready for the question?" If no one rises, he once more states the question as already described, and puts it to vote.

One of the commonest forms of putting the question (after it has been stated) is this: "As many as are in favor of the motion will say *aye;* those opposed will say *no.*" Another one is as follows: "Those in favor of the motion will hold up the right hand; those opposed will manifest it by the same sign."†

---

* The question, in some societies, is more usually: "Are there any remarks?" or, "Are there any further remarks?"

† See §§ 38, 46-48, 54 for examples of various ways of stating and putting questions, and page 10 for peculiar forms.

PART III.

MISCELLANEOUS.

66. The Right of Deliberative Assemblies to Punish their Members.

A deliberative assembly has the inherent right to make and enforce its own laws and punish an offender — the extreme penalty, however, being expulsion from its own body. When expelled, if the assembly is a permanent society, it has a right, for its own protection, to give public notice that the person has ceased to be a member of that society.

But it has no right to go beyond what is necessary for self-protection and publish the charges against the member. In a case where a member of a society was expelled, and an officer of the society published, by their order, a statement of the grave charges upon which he had been found guilty, the expelled member recovered damages from the officer in a suit for libel, the Court holding that the truth of the charges did not affect the case.

67. Right of an Assembly to Eject any one from its Place of Meeting.

Every deliberative assembly has the right to decide who may be present during its session; and when the assembly, either by a rule or by a vote, decides that a certain person shall not remain in the room, it is the duty of the Chairman to enforce the rule or order, using whatever force is necessary to eject the party.

The Chairman can detail members to remove the person, without calling upon the police. If, however, in enforcing the order, any one uses harsher treatment than is necessary to remove the person, the courts have held that he, and he alone, is liable to prosecution, just the same as a policeman would be under similar circumstances. However badly the man may be abused while being removed from the room, neither the Chairman nor the society are liable for damages, as, in ordering his removal, they did not exceed their legal rights.

68. Rights of Ecclesiastical Tribunals.

Many of our deliberative assemblies are ecclesiastical bodies, and it is important to know how much respect will be paid to their decisions by the civil courts.

A church became divided, and each party claimed to be the church, and therefore entitled to the church property. The case was taken into the civil courts, and finally, on appeal, to the U. S. Supreme Court, which held the case under advisement for one year, and then reversed the decision of the State Court, because it conflicted with the decision of the highest ecclesiastical court that had acted upon the case. The Supreme Court, in rendering its decision, laid down the broad principle that, when a local church is but a part of a larger and more general organization or denomination, the court will accept the decision of the highest ecclesiastical tribunal to which the case has been carried within that general church organization as final, and will not inquire into the justice or injustice of its decree as between the parties before it. The officers, the ministers, the members, or the church body, which the highest judiciary of the denomination recognizes, the court will recognize. Whom that body expels or cuts off, the court will hold to be no longer members of that church.

69. Trial of Members of Societies.

Every deliberative assembly, having the right to purify its own body, must therefore have the right to investigate the character of its members.   It can require any of them to testify in the case, under pain of expulsion if they refuse.

When the charge is against the member's character, it is usually referred to a committee of investigation or discipline, or to some standing committee, to report upon. Some societies have standing committees, whose duty it is to report cases for discipline whenever any are known to them.

In either case the committee investigate the matter and report to the society.   This report need not go into details, but should contain their recommendations as to what action the society should take, and should usually close with resolutions covering the case, so that there is no need for any one to offer any additional resolutions upon it.   The ordinary resolutions, where the member is recommended to be expelled, are (1) to fix the time to which the society shall adjourn; and (2) to instruct the clerk to cite the member to appear before the society at this adjourned meeting to show cause why he should not be expelled, upon the following charges which should then be given.

After charges are preferred against a member,

and the assembly has ordered that he be cited to appear for trial, he is theoretically under arrest, and is deprived of all the rights of membership until his case is disposed of. Without his consent no member should be tried at the same meeting at which the charges are preferred, excepting when the charges relate to something done in that meeting.

The clerk should send the accused a written notice to appear before the society at the time appointed, and should at the same time furnish him with a copy of the charges. A failure to obey the summons is generally cause enough for summary expulsion.

At the appointed meeting what may be called the trial takes place. Frequently the only evidence required against the member is the report of the committee. After it has been read and any additional evidence offered that the committee may see fit to introduce, the accused should be allowed to make an explanation and introduce witnesses, if he so desires. Either party should be allowed to cross-examine the other's witnesses and introduce rebutting testimony. When the evidence is all in, the accused should retire from the room, and the society deliberate upon the question, and finally act by a vote upon the question of expulsion, or other punishment proposed. No member should be expelled by less than a two-thirds* vote — a quorum voting.

In acting upon the case, it must be borne in mind that there is a vast distinction between the evidence necessary to convict in a civil court and that required to convict in an ordinary society or ecclesiastical body. A notorious pickpocket could not even be arrested, much less convicted by a civil court, simply on the ground of being commonly known as a pickpocket; while such evidence would convict and expel him from any ordinary society.

The moral conviction of the truth of the charge is all that is necessary, in an ecclesiastical or other deliberative body, to find the accused guilty of the charges.

If the trial is liable to be long and troublesome, or of a very delicate nature, the member is frequently cited to appear before a committee, instead of the society, for trial. In this case the committee report to the society the result of their trial of the case, with resolutions

---

* The U. S. Constitution [Art. 1, Sec. 5] provides that each house of Congress may, "with the concurrence of two-thirds, expel a member."

covering the punishment which they recommend the society to adopt. When the committee's report is read, the accused should be permitted to make his statement of the case, the committee being allowed to reply. The accused then retires from the room, and the society act upon the resolutions submitted by the committee. The members of the committee should vote upon the case the same as other members.

If the accused wishes counsel at his trial, it is usual to allow it, provided the counsel is a member of the society in good standing. Should the counsel be guilty of improper conduct during the trial, the society can refuse to hear him, and can also punish him.

70. Call of the House.

The object of a call of the house is to compel the attendance of absent members, and is allowable only in assemblies that have the power to compel the attendance of absentees. It is usual to provide that when no quorum is present, a small number [one-fifth of the members elect in Congress*] can order a call of

---

* In the early history of our Congress a call of the house required a day's notice, and in the English Parliament it is usual to order that the call shall be made on a certain day in the future,

the house. To prevent this privilege from being used improperly, it is well to provide that when the call is made the members cannot adjourn or dispense with further proceedings in the call until a quorum is obtained. A rule like the following would answer for city councils and other similar bodies that have the power to enforce attendance:

Rule. When no quorum is present, — members may order a call of the house and compel the attendance of absent members. After the call is ordered, a motion to adjourn, or to dispense with further proceedings in the call, cannot be entertained until a quorum is present, or until the Sergeant-at-Arms reports that in his opinion no quorum can be obtained on that day.

If no quorum is present a call of the house takes precedence of everything, even reading the minutes, except the motion to adjourn, and only requires in its favor the number specified

---

usually not over ten days afterwards, though it has been as long as six weeks afterwards. The object of this is to give notice so that all the members may be present on that day, when important business is to come before the house. In Congress a call of the house is only used now when no quorum is present, and as soon as a quorum appears it is usual to dispense with further proceedings in the call, and this is in order at any stage of the proceedings. In some of our legislative bodies proceedings in the call cannot be dispensed with except a majority of the members elect vote in favor of so doing. In Congress it is customary afterwards to remit the fees that have been assessed.

in the rule. If a quorum is present a call should rank with questions of privilege [§ 12], requiring a majority vote for its adoption, and if rejected it should not be renewed, while a quorum is present, at that meeting [see first note to § 42]. After a call is ordered, until further proceedings in the call are dispensed with, no motion is in order except to adjourn and a motion relating to the call, so that a recess could not be taken by unanimous consent. An adjournment puts an end to all proceedings in the call, except that the assembly before adjournment, if a quorum is present, can order such members as are already arrested to make their excuses at an adjourned meeting.

Proceedings in a Call of the House. When the call is ordered the clerk calls the roll of members alphabetically, noting the absentees; he then calls over again the names of absentees, when excuses* can be made; after this the doors are locked, no one being permitted to leave, and an order similar in form to the fol-

---

* It is usual in Congress to excuse those who have "paired off," that is, two members on opposite sides of the pending question who have agreed that both will stay away. In order to "pair off," the absence of both parties must not affect the result, which would rarely be the case in municipal bodies like those under consideration.

lowing is adopted: "That the Sergeant-at-Arms take into custody, and bring to the bar of the House, such of its members as are absent without the leave of the House." A warrant signed by the presiding officer and attested by the clerk, with a list of absentees attached, is then given to the Sergeant-at-Arms,* who immediately proceeds to arrest the absentees. When he appears with members under arrest, he proceeds to the Chairman's desk (being announced by the doorkeeper in large bodies), followed by the arrested members, and makes his return. The Chairman arraigns each member separately, and asks what excuse he has to offer for being absent from the sittings of the assembly without its leave. The member states his excuse, and a motion is made that he be discharged from custody and admitted to his seat either without payment of fees or after paying the fees. Until a member has paid the fees assessed against him he cannot vote or be recognized by the Chair for any purpose.

---

* " It shall be the duty of the Sergeant-at-Arms to attend the House during its sittings; to aid in the enforcement of order, under the direction of the Speaker; to execute the commands of the House from time to time; together with all such process, issued by authority thereof, as shall be directed to him by the Speaker" (Rule 22 H. R.) The words "Sergeant-at-Arms" can be replaced in the order by " Chief of Police," or whatever officer is to serve the process.

INDEX.

The figures from 1 to 45 refer to sections in Part I. Always consult the Table of Rules, p. 8, for information about any particular motion. A complete list of motions will be found in the Index, under the title, "Motions, list of." The arrangement of the work can be most easily seen by examining the Table of Contents [pp. 3–6]; its plan is explained in the Introduction, pp. 16–19.